For Annie

First published in Great Britain in 2004 by
MAINSTREAM PUBLISHING COMPANY
(EDINBURGH) LTD
7 Albany Street
Edinburgh EH1 3UG

ISBN 1 84018 533 3

A catalogue record for this book is available
from the British Library

Typeset in Allise and Van Dijck

Printed in Great Britain by
Antony Rowe Ltd., Chippenham, Wiltshire

Ann,

You have plenty of time
to figure this out!

Love Jan.                    September 2006

ALSO BY JANE RIDDER-PATRICK

*A Handbook of Medical Astrology*
*Shaping Your Future* (Series of 12 titles)
*Shaping Your Relationships* (Series of 12 titles)

*The Zodiac Code series*

# THE
# LIBRA
ENIGMA

*Cracking the Code*

JANE RIDDER-PATRICK

MAINSTREAM
PUBLISHING
EDINBURGH AND LONDON

# Contents

ONE       The Truth of Astrology     7

TWO       The Symbolism of Libra     16

THREE     The Heart of the Sun     20

FOUR      The Drama of Being a Libran     24

FIVE       The Libra Temperament     28

SIX        Aspects of the Sun     41

SEVEN    Meeting Your Moon     48

EIGHT     Mercury – It's All in the Mind     68

NINE      Venus – At Your Pleasure     77

TEN        Famous Libra Birthdays     86

ELEVEN   Finding Your Sun, Moon, Mercury
and Venus Signs     94

The Libra Workbook     119

Resources     126

Your Libran Friends     127

Sign Summaries     128

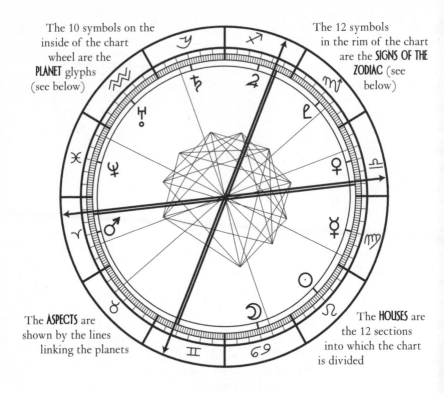

The 10 symbols on the inside of the chart wheel are the **PLANET** glyphs (see below)

The 12 symbols in the rim of the chart are the **SIGNS OF THE ZODIAC** (see below)

The **ASPECTS** are shown by the lines linking the planets

The **HOUSES** are the 12 sections into which the chart is divided

## A Sample Birth Chart

| Sign | Ruler | Sign | Ruler |
|------|-------|------|-------|
| Aries ♈ | Mars ♂ | Libra ♎ | Venus ♀ |
| Taurus ♉ | Venus ♀ | Scorpio ♏ | Pluto ♇ |
| Gemini ♊ | Mercury ☿ | Sagittarius ♐ | Jupiter ♃ |
| Cancer ♋ | Moon ☽ | Capricorn ♑ | Saturn ♄ |
| Leo ♌ | Sun ☉ | Aquarius ♒ | Uranus ♅ |
| Virgo ♍ | Mercury ☿ | Pisces ♓ | Neptune ♆ |

# ONE

# The Truth of Astrology

MOST PEOPLE'S FIRST EXPERIENCE OF ASTROLOGY IS THROUGH newspapers and magazines. This is a mixed blessing for astrology's reputation – writing an astrology column to any degree of accuracy is a tough, many would say impossible, challenge. The astrologer has to try to say something meaningful about conditions that affect every single person belonging to the same sign, over a very short period of time, in a scant handful of words. The miracle is that some talented astrologers do manage to get across a tantalising whiff of the real thing and keep readers coming back for more of what most of us are hungry for – self-knowledge and reassurance about the future. The downside of the popularity of these columns is that many people think that all astrology is a branch of the entertainment industry and is limited to light-hearted fortune-telling. This is far from the truth.

## What Astrology Can Offer
Serious astrology is one of the most sophisticated tools available to help us understand ourselves and the world

around us. It gives us a language and a framework to examine and describe – quite literally – *anything* under the Sun, from countries to companies, from money markets to medical matters. Its most common application, however, is in helping people to understand themselves better using their own unique birth charts. Astrology has two main functions. One is to describe the traits and tendencies of whatever it is that is being examined, whether this is a state, a software company or someone's psyche. The other is to give an astonishingly accurate timetable for important changes within that entity. In the chapters that follow, we'll be using astrology to investigate the psychology of the innermost part of your personality, taking a look at what drives, inspires and motivates you.

Astrology uses an ancient system of symbols to describe profound truths about the nature of life on earth, truths that cannot be weighed and measured, but ones we recognise nevertheless, and that touch and move us at a deep level. By linking mythology and mathematics, astrology bridges the gap between our inner lives and our outer experiences, between mind and matter, between poetry and science.

## Fate and Free Will

Some people think that astrology is all about foretelling the future, the implication being that everything is predestined and that we have no say in how our lives take shape. None of that is true. We are far from being helpless victims of fate. Everything that happens to us at any given time is the result of past choices. These choices may have been our own, or made by other people. They could even have been made long ago before we, or even our grandparents, were born. It is not always possible to prevent processes that were set in motion in the past from coming to their logical conclusions as events that we then have to deal with. We are, however, all free to decide how to react to whatever is presented to us at every moment of our lives.

Your destiny is linked directly with your personality because the choices you make, consciously or unconsciously, depend largely on your own natural inclinations. It is these inclinations that psychological astrology describes. You can live out every single part of your chart in a constructive or a less constructive way. For instance, if you have Aries strong in your chart, action and initiative will play a major role in your life. It is your choice whether you express yourself aggressively or assertively, heroically or selfishly, and also whether you are the doer or the done-to. Making the right choices is important because every decision has consequences – and what you give out, sooner or later, you get back. If you don't know and understand yourself, you are 'fated' to act according to instinct and how your life experiences have conditioned you. By revealing how you are wired up temperamentally, astrology can highlight alternatives to blind knee-jerk reactions, which often make existing problems worse. This self-knowledge can allow you to make more informed free-will choices, and so help you create a better and more successful future for yourself.

## Astrology and Prediction
Astrology cannot predict specific events based on your birth chart. That kind of prediction belongs to clairvoyance and divination. These specialities, when practised by gifted and responsible individuals, can give penetrating insights into events that are likely to happen in the future if matters proceed along their present course.

The real benefit of seeing into the future is that if we don't like what could happen if we carry on the way we're going, we can take steps either to prevent it or to lessen its impact. Rarely is the future chiselled out in stone. There are many possible futures. What you feed with your attention grows. Using your birth chart, a competent astrologer can map out, for years in advance, major turning points, showing which areas of your life will be affected at these times and the kind of change that will be taking place. This information gives answers to the questions that most clients ask in one way or another: 'Why me, why this and why now?' If you accept responsibility for facing what needs to be done at the appropriate time, and doing it, you can change the course of your life for the better.

## Astrology and the Soul

What is sometimes called the soul and its purpose is a mystery much more profound than astrology. Most of us have experienced 'chance' meetings and apparent 'tragedies' which have affected the direction of our entire lives. There is an intelligence at work that is infinitely wiser and more powerful than the will or wishes of our small, egocentric personalities. This force, whatever name we give it – Universal Wisdom, the Inner Guide, the Self, a guardian angel – steers us into exactly the right conditions for our souls' growth. Astrology can pinpoint the turning points in the course of your destiny and describe the equipment that you have at your disposal for serving, or resisting, the soul's purpose. That equipment is your personality.

## Who Are You?

You are no doubt aware of your many good qualities as well as your rather more resistible ones that you might prefer to keep firmly under wraps. Maybe you have wondered why it is that one part of your personality seems to want to do one thing while another part is stubbornly intent on doing the exact opposite. Have you ever wished that you could crack the code that holds the secrets of what makes you – and significant others – behave in the complex way you do? The good news is that you can, with the help of your astrological birth chart, sometimes known as your horoscope.

Just as surely as your DNA identifies you and distinguishes you from everyone else, as well as encoding your peculiarities and potential, your birth chart reveals the unique 'DNA fingerprinting' of your personality. This may seem a staggering claim, but it is one that those who have experienced serious astrology will endorse, so let's take a closer look at what a birth chart is.

## Your Birth Chart

Your birth chart is a simplified diagram of the positions of the planets, as seen from the place of your birth, at the moment you took your first independent breath. Critics have said that astrology is obviously nonsense because birth charts are drawn up as if the Sun and all the planets moved round the Earth.

We know in our minds that the Earth moves round the Sun, but that doesn't stop us seeing the Sun rise in the east in the morning and move across the sky to set in the west in the evening. This is an optical illusion. In the same way, we know (or at least most of us know) that we are not really the centre of the universe, but that doesn't stop us experiencing ourselves as being at the focal point of our own personal worlds. It is impossible to live life in any other way. It is the strength, not weakness, of astrology that it describes from your own unique viewpoint how you, as an individual, experience life.

## Erecting Your Chart

To draw up a full birth chart you need three pieces of information – the date, time and place of your birth. With your birth date alone you can find the positions of all the planets (except sometimes the Moon) to a good enough degree of accuracy to reveal a great deal of important information about you. If you have the time and place of birth, too, an astrologer can calculate your Ascendant or Rising Sign and the houses of your chart – see below. The Ascendant is a bit like the front door of your personality and describes your general outlook on life. (If you know your Ascendant sign, you might like to read more about its characteristics in the book on that sign in this series.)

The diagram on page 6 shows what a birth chart looks like. Most people find it pretty daunting at first sight but it actually breaks down into only four basic units – the planets, the signs, the aspects and the houses.

## The Planets

Below is a simple list of what the planets represent.

| PLANET | REPRESENTS YOUR URGE TO |
|---|---|
| ☉ The Sun | express your identity |
| ☽ The Moon | feel nurtured and safe |
| ☿ Mercury | make connections |
| ♀ Venus | attract what you love |
| ♂ Mars | assert your will |
| ♃ Jupiter | find meaning in life |
| ♄ Saturn | achieve your ambitions |
| ♅ Uranus | challenge tradition |
| ♆ Neptune | serve an ideal |
| ♇ Pluto | eliminate, transform and survive |

The planets represent the main psychological drives that every single one of us has. The exact way in which we express these drives is not fixed from birth but develops and evolves throughout our lives, both consciously and unconsciously. In this book we will be examining in detail four of these planets – your Sun, Moon, Mercury and Venus. These are the bodies that are right at the heart of our solar system. They correspond, in psychological astrology, to the core of your personality and represent how you express yourself, what motivates you emotionally, how you use your mind and what brings you pleasure.

## The Signs
The signs your planets are in show how you tend to express your inner drives. For example, if your Mars is in the action sign of Aries, you will assert yourself pretty directly, pulling no punches. If your Venus is in secretive Scorpio, you will attract, and also be attracted to, emotionally intense relationships. There is a summary of all of the signs on p. 128.

## The Aspects
Aspects are important relationships between planets and whether your inner characteristics clash with or complement each other depends largely on whether or not they are in aspect and whether that aspect is an easy or a challenging one. In Chapter Six we'll be looking at some challenging aspects to the Sun.

## The Houses
Your birth chart is divided into 12 slices, called houses, each of which is associated with a particular area of life, such as friendships, travel or home life. If, for example, you have your Uranus in the house of career, you are almost

certainly a bit of a maverick at work. If you have your Neptune in the house of partnership, you are likely to idealise your husband, wife or business partner.

## The Nature of Time

Your birth chart records a moment in time and space, like a still from a movie – the movie being the apparent movement of the planets round the earth. We all know that time is something that can be measured in precise units, which are always the same, like seconds, months and centuries. But if you stop to reflect for a moment, you'll also recognise that time doesn't always feel the same. Twenty minutes waiting for a bus on a cold, rainy day can seem like a miserable eternity, while the same amount of time spent with someone you love can pass in a flash. As Einstein would say – that's relativity.

There are times in history when something significant seems to be in the air, but even when nothing momentous is happening the quality of time shifts into different 'moods' from moment to moment. Your birth chart is impregnated with the qualities of the time when you were born. For example, people who were born in the mid-to-late 1960s, when society was undergoing major disruptive changes, carry those powerful energies within them and their personalities reflect, in many ways, the turmoil of those troubled and exciting times. Now, as adults, the choices that those individuals make, based on their own inner conflicts and compulsions, will help shape the future of society for better or worse. And so it goes on through the generations.

## Seed Meets Soil

There is no such thing as a good or bad chart, nor is any one sign better or worse than another. There are simply 12 different, but equally important, life focuses. It's useful to keep in mind the fact that the chart of each one of us is made up of all the signs of the zodiac. This means that we'll act out, or experience, *every* sign somewhere in our lives. It is true, however, that some individual charts are more challenging than others; but the greater the challenge, the greater the potential for achievement and self-understanding.

In gardening terms, your chart is a bit like the picture on a seed packet. It shows what you could become. If the seeds are of poppies, there's no way you'll get petunias, but external conditions will affect how they grow. With healthy soil, a friendly climate and green-fingered gardeners, the plants have an excellent chance of flourishing. With poor soil, a harsh climate or constant neglect, the seeds will be forced to struggle. This is not always a disadvantage. They can become hardy and adapt, finding new and creative ways of evolving and thriving under more extreme conditions than the plant that was well cared for. It's the same with your chart. The environment you were raised in may have been friendly or hostile to your nature and it will have done much to shape your life until now. Using the insights of astrology to affirm who you are, you can, as an adult, provide your own ideal conditions, become your own best gardener and live out more fully – and successfully – your own highest potential.

# TWO

# The Symbolism of Libra

WE CAN LEARN A GREAT DEAL ABOUT LIBRA BY LOOKING AT the symbolism and the myths and legends associated with it. These carry more information than plain facts alone and hint at the deeper meanings and significance of the sign.

Libra's glyph is two horizontal lines running in parallel, with a half-circle raised in the centre of the top one. Libra is associated with the westerly direction, and the lines of the glyph can be seen as the setting sun, half of it still visible above the horizon while the other half has sunk out of sight, at the point when day and night are equally balanced. You, as a Libran, are often in the position of trying to hold the balance between two seemingly irreconcilable opposites. The glyph can also be seen as a bird with outstretched wings flying over the earth, parallel to it but not touching it, and so enjoying a 'bird's eye view' of the whole scene. Librans are known for their ability to rise above purely worldly concerns and to see, in a detached way, the connections between everyone and everything. Sometimes, though, you may prefer to stay up in the clouds with your lofty ideas, making you appear rather naive and out of touch with the hard realities of life.

The glyph's similarity to a traditional bridge refers to the Libran gift of diplomacy, which helps establish a dialogue between people who may be at odds with each other, or have opposing agendas. Another way of interpreting the image is as an open book lying face downwards, highlighting the tendency of Librans to play it formally, by the book, both in law and in love. Finally, the glyph can also represent a yoke. Libra is the sign of partnerships, both personal and professional, where two people are yoked together by a mutually agreed contract. Alliances bring both burdens and responsibilities but, if both pull together, great feats can be achieved. Esoterically, it hints at the true purpose of all relationships, which is to demonstrate that love is the law of the universe.

## Libra the Scales

Libra is the only sign of the zodiac that is not represented by a living creature, underlining its emphasis on abstract ideas, rather than the instincts. The symbol of Libra is a pair of old-fashioned scales, with two pans hanging from a bar and a pivot exactly in the middle. When something is put in one pan, something else of exactly the same weight must be put in the other if the scales are to balance. As a Libran, you like to weigh up all aspects of a matter carefully, before finally coming to a fair and balanced assessment. Every new development unbalances the pans, so the scales are rarely at rest or in equilibrium, forcing you to make constant adjustments to keep the system in relative harmony.

Libra comes from the Latin meaning balance, or scales, and it is the word for the Roman pound weight as well.

From it comes the contraction for the British pound, which is lb., and also the unit of value, the pound sterling, and the name for Italian currency, the lira. Libra is associated both with weighing and measuring to ensure that justice is done, and also with relative values, of which money is the common unit of exchange. In ancient China the annual standardisation of weights and measures apparently took place when the Sun was in Libra.

On the roof of the Old Bailey Law Courts in London there is a golden statue representing the goddess of Justice, blindfolded to show the law's impartiality to rank, creed or colour. With arms outstretched, she holds the scales of Libra in one hand and in the other the sword of Mars, ruler of Aries, Libra's opposite sign. This shows that the law demands both the weighing up of evidence and also vigorous action to enforce it. The Scales of Libra also refer to one of the great spiritual laws of life, the Law of Equilibrium, sometimes known as the Law of Karma: action and reaction are equal and opposite, or 'As you do, so shall it be done unto you.'

## The Ruler of Libra

Like Taurus, Libra is ruled by Venus, the goddess of love and battles. Venus was also known as Aphrodite, and earlier Innana and Ishtar. Breathtakingly beautiful and seductive, she had many lovers and admirers. She held the key to all the arts of civilisation, like architecture, mathematics, dancing and song. Her greatest skill, however, was one which she earned only in maturity, that of decision-making. All of these areas are familiar territory to Librans: beauty, culture, decisions and – yes – battles. When it comes to beauty, for Libra, in contrast to Taurus, the emphasis is more on the cultivated, rather than the natural, variety.

## Libra in Myth and Legend

Ancient Egyptians believed that after death every soul had to appear before Thoth, the god of wisdom. The heart, representing the conscience, was weighed in the scales against the feather of Maat, goddess of law, truth and justice. If these were exactly balanced, the person was allowed to join the gods in the Fields of Peace. If not, the soul, after a brief rest, had to return to earth for the further experience needed to bring it to perfect balance and beauty. Michaelmas, the feast of St Michael, falls at the beginning of Libra. St Michael, one of the archangels, was, like Thoth, a divine messenger and executor of God's judgements. As well as slaying the dragon, which represents the evils of the world, his task was to weigh souls as part of the Last Judgement.

## The Season of Libra

Libra begins at the autumn equinox, when day and night are of equal length. Harvest has been gathered in and the heat, and holiday season, of summer is over. It is a time of great beauty as leaves change colour and then start to fall, in preparation for the long winter rest. The university year begins and, in the community, evening classes start up, offering opportunities for self-cultivation. When the Sun enters Libra it has travelled halfway round the zodiac and its return journey now begins. During the following six months, each sign the Sun passes through complements the one opposite. This echoes the Libran themes of balance and coupling.

# THREE

# The Heart of the Sun

⊙ THE GLYPH FOR THE SUN IS A PERFECT CIRCLE WITH A DOT in the centre and symbolises our dual nature – earthly and eternal. The circle stands for the boundary of the personality, which distinguishes and separates each individual from every other individual, for it is our differences from other people that make us unique, not our similarities. The dot in the centre indicates the mysterious 'divine spark' within us and the potential for becoming conscious of who we truly are, where we have come from and what we may become.

## The Meaning of the Sun

Each of your planets represents a different strand of your personality. The Sun is often reckoned to be the most important factor of your whole birth chart. It describes your sense of identity, and the sign that the Sun was in when you were born, your Sun sign, along with its house position and any aspects to other planets, shows how you express and develop that identity.

## Your Role in Life

Each of the signs is associated with certain roles that can be played in an infinite number of ways. Take one of the roles of Aries, which is the warrior. A warrior can cover anything from Attila the Hun, who devastated vast stretches of Europe with his deliberate violence, to an eco-warrior, battling to save the environment. The role, warrior, is the same; the motivation and actions are totally different. You can live out every part of your personality in four main ways – as creator, destroyer, onlooker or victim. How you act depends on who you choose to be from the endless variations possible from the symbolism of each of your planets, but most particularly your Sun. And you do have a choice; not all Geminis are irresponsible space cadets nor is every Scorpio a sex-crazed sadist. This book aims to paint a picture of what some of your choices might be and show what choices, conscious or unconscious, some well-known people of your sign have made.

Your upbringing will have helped shape what you believe about yourself and out of those beliefs comes, automatically, behaviour to match. For example, if you believe you are a victim, you will behave like one and the world will happily oblige by victimising you. If you see yourself as a carer, life will present you with plenty to care for – and often to care about, too. If you identify yourself as an adventurer, you'll spot opportunities at every corner. If you're a winner, then you'll tend to succeed. Shift the way that you see yourself and your whole world shifts, too.

## Your Vocation

Your Sun describes your major life focus. This is not always a career. As the poet Milton said: 'They also serve who only stand and wait.' It is impossible to tell from your Sun sign exactly what your calling is – there are people of all signs occupied in practically every area of life. What is important is not so much *what* you do, but the way that you do it and it is this – how you express yourself – that your Sun describes. If you spend most of your time working at an occupation or living in a situation where you can't give expression to the qualities of your Sun, or which forces you to go against the grain of your Sun's natural inclinations, then you're likely to live a life of quiet, or possibly even noisy, desperation.

## On Whose Authority

Your personality, which your birth chart maps, is like a sensitive instrument that will resonate only to certain frequencies – those that are similar to its own. Your Sun shows the kind of authority that will strike a chord with you, either positively or negatively, because it is in harmony with yours. It can show how you relate to people in authority, especially your father. (It is the Moon that usually shows the relationship with your mother and home.) In adult life it can throw light onto the types of bosses you are likely to come across, and also how you could react to them. It is a major part of the maturing process to take responsibility for expressing your own authority wisely. When you do so, many of your problems with external authorities diminish or even disappear.

In a woman's chart the Sun can also describe the kind of husband she chooses. This is partly because, traditionally, a husband had legal authority over his wife. It is also because, especially in the early years of a marriage, many women choose to pour their energies into homemaking and supporting their husbands' work in the world, rather than their own, and so his career becomes her career. As a

Libran, you may find that your father, boss or husband shows either the positive or negative traits of Libra or, as is usually the case, a mixture of both – courteous, fair and co-operative or frivolous, indecisive and over-anxious to please.

## Born on the Cusp

If you were born near the beginning or end of Libra, you may know that your birthday falls on the cusp, or meeting point, of two signs. The Sun, however, can only be in one sign or the other. You can find out for sure which sign your Sun is in by checking the tables on pp. 97–8.

# FOUR

# The Drama of Being a Libran

EACH SIGN IS ASSOCIATED WITH A CLUSTER OF ROLES THAT HAVE their own core drama or storyline. Being born is a bit like arriving in the middle of an ongoing play and slipping into a certain part. How we play our characters is powerfully shaped in early life by having to respond to the input of the other actors around us – the people that make up our families and communities. As the play of our lives unfolds, we usually become aware that there are themes which tend to repeat themselves. We may ask ourselves questions like 'Why do I always end up with all the work / caught up in fights / with partners who mistreat me / in dead-end jobs/ successful but unhappy . . .?' or whatever. Interestingly, I've found that people are less likely to question the wonderful things that happen to them again and again.

The good news is that once we recognise the way we have been playing our roles, we can then use our free-will choice to do some creative re-scripting, using the same character in more constructive scenarios. Even better news is that if we change, the other people in our dramas have got to make some alterations, too. If you refuse to respond to the same old cues in the customary ways, they are going to have to get creative, too.

A core role of Libra is the architect. An architect – in the word's broadest sense – means someone who designs and oversees the implementation of a grand plan of any kind. Looking at the work of an architect, in its narrower sense, as a designer of buildings, sheds a lot of light on how Libra operates. An architect works in partnership with a client. He, or she, has to work with the client's ideas and preferences, but without compromising architectural principles, building regulations or his or her convictions of how matters should proceed. The client, who is, after all, the one funding the project, has to be kept sweet throughout all of the delicate initial negotiations. Costing is one of the biggest nightmares of the task because of future variables. The client has to be reassured that the architect is providing value for money, while the latter has to charge a fair price for the work provided, which is often enormously time-consuming, yet, to the client, invisible.

An architect has to work to create harmony in many areas, often simultaneously. Sorting out squabbles among contractors and snags in the plans demands the skills of a diplomat – and the foresight to prepare for hitches and make instant adjustments. Remember the scales of Libra. A tiny alteration on one side puts the pans out of balance. The task of paying close and constant attention to any shift in the equilibrium, and applying counterbalancing measures, parallels the never-ending balancing act that is your life as a Libran.

The architect, working as closely as possible to the client's specifications, first needs to come up with a plan, as before anything can come into material form it must first be conceived in the mind as an idea. Each of the measurements in the design must be in correct relationship with every other one. If the proportions are wrong, the final appearance will suffer. Also, the plans must take into consideration the intended purpose of the construction. An exquisite building not fit for its function is simply a costly white elephant. Most important of all, the design must work when put into practice. In the Middle Ages, despite the proportions being right, many buildings, notably Beauvais Cathedral in France, collapsed because of the gap between abstract theory and the laws of the material world. Bridging this gap is just as vital today. Despite its superb design, the Millennium Footbridge over the Thames in London had to be closed almost immediately for adjustments because it wobbled so alarmingly when people actually walked over it. As a Libran, you too have the difficult task of reconciling ideas and actuality to produce a harmonious outcome which, when successful, makes a pleasing contribution to human civilisation.

Other roles associated with Libra all involve relationships – between people, ideas or materials. They are the designer, planner, diplomat, peacemaker, judge, arbitrator, general, partner and courtesan. Negative roles are the schemer and flatterer, where the inner demons of desire, vanity or laziness overwhelm the personality and fair Libra turns foul, like Snow White's wicked stepmother.

The life of most Librans is touched, at some stage, by challenge or crisis concerning relationships. That includes enemies, who are partners in conflict, as well as business and romantic partners. For some it is loss, or the threat of loss, while others are faced with the equally unsettling experience of finding themselves having to confront their own fear of confrontation and learning to be fair to themselves.

How you choose to see your role will determine your behaviour. The following chapter describes some typical Libran behaviour. Remember, though, that there is no such thing as a person who is all Libra and nothing but Libra. You are much more complicated than that and other parts of your chart will modify, or may even seem to contradict, the single, but central, strand of your personality which is your Sun sign. These other sides of your nature will add colour and contrast and may restrict or reinforce your basic Libran identity. They won't, however, cancel out the challenges you face as a Libran.

# FIVE

# The Libra Temperament

WITH YOUR PASSION FOR FAIRNESS, YOU UNDERSTAND THAT everyone's ideas and opinions deserve a fair hearing, even if those views do conflict with your own. Your idea of being agreeable means that you'll appear to agree with just about everyone you meet – for as long as that meeting lasts. A moment later, though, could find you in agreement with someone else whose notions are diametrically opposite to those of the person you've just left. This can make you seem like a weather vane whose direction changes with the wind, but your primary focus is actually on creating harmony with others through sharing common ground, rather than on emphasising where you differ.

## Indecisions, Indecisions

There's an old astrological saying that you can always tell Librans from the cleft backsides they get from sitting on the fence. Coming to a decision can be hard for you, partly because you want to make the right one and, ideally, you'd like to please everybody, which is clearly impossible. You realise, too, that there are seldom simple solutions, only compromises. So you'll rarely act without consulting others and getting their input and feedback, even though often you know perfectly well what you want to do, and go on to do it anyway. Being aware that saying 'yes' to one person means saying 'no' to another, your fear is that the one you refuse will dislike you and maybe even attack you, either of which is your idea of a nightmare. So you prefer to share decision-making, or even to pass the buck, rather than pressing on alone. That way you dodge responsibility and the full brunt of any negative consequences.

You may also put off taking action until it's too late, trying to keep all your options open. But even here you can't escape, because not making a choice is a choice in itself, with consequences sometimes much worse than what would have happened if you'd grasped the nettle firmly in the first place. Some Librans are chronic ditherers and hoverers, ready to draw back and so remain forever passively at the mercy of other people's choices. Every sign can learn a great deal from the one opposite, which in your case is Aries. Add some spontaneity, decisive action and up-front self-interest to your courtesy and tact, and the world could be your oyster.

## No Offence

You'll do all you can to avoid conflict and when it comes to emotional confrontation you can be charmingly evasive. Ideally, you'd love to have no enemies, but this can be taken too far. Sometimes, in your willingness to cooperate and compromise, you'll go much further than just meeting the other halfway, and will abandon your own position so as not to rock the boat. As many Librans have found to their cost, that's too high a price to pay for peace. Your biggest breakthrough comes when you accept the unpalatable fact that there will always be some people who will like you and some people who won't, regardless of how much honey you drip-feed them. Taking a deep breath and holding firm to your principles, no matter how unpopular it makes you, is your gateway to freedom, maturity and unshakeable integrity. By confronting your worst fears you'll have gained poise and earned freedom from anxiety, for you'll have found that not only do you survive, but you positively thrive. You'll then experience the joy of choosing the truth, whatever the risk, and speaking up and acting for whatever you believe is right, which are Libra's finest qualities.

### It's A Beautiful Life

You've a gift for spotting the good points in people and situations and presenting them tastefully in the best possible light. Disharmony, ugliness and vulgarity, both in surroundings and relationships, can be unbearably painful for you. Unpleasantness or getting your hands dirty – in any sense of the word – you'd much rather avoid. You hate temper tantrums, hysterics and heavy emotions and may naively believe that troubled issues can, and should, be resolved by nice, quiet, civilised communication. Some Librans can't even bear films and books where the tension mounts too much. Libran writer P.G. Wodehouse said that his work was about making a musical comedy without music, and ignoring real life altogether. Because you find life's brutalities scary and offensive, you may retreat into your ivory tower, and pull up the drawbridge, but refusing to deal with harsh realities won't make them go away.

### Love Thy Neighbour

The biblical sayings 'Do unto others as you would be done by' and 'Love your neighbour as yourself' are ones that resonate with most Librans. Remember, though, it's a balanced equation, and doesn't say 'Love your neighbour and ignore yourself.' The great Libran Indian leader Mahatma Gandhi had eight clear guidelines about treating opponents fairly to bring about the peace that is your passion. These read like the prescription for being a perfect Libran. He taught his followers:

- Don't be violent or hostile.
- Try to gain your opponent's trust.
- Never humiliate people.
- Be willing to make visible sacrifices if you want them to do so too.
- Cooperate with them in non-disputed areas to strengthen the relationship.
- Show that you trust and expect them to be their best selves.
- Keep up personal contact to hold open the avenues of communication.
- Imagine yourself in their position and develop goodwill, patience and understanding of their motives.

Like Gandhi, through genuine empathy and tact you can often achieve what would have been completely impossible by direct or bulldozing tactics.

## Two in One

Libran women tend to combine the feminine graces with a masculine mind and will. The French president François Mitterand once said of Margaret Thatcher that she had the eyes of Caligula and the mouth of Marilyn Monroe. Libran men, on the other hand, tend to combine masculine drive and confidence with feminine intuition and gentleness. Some are even, quite mistakenly, thought to be gay because of their attractiveness and grace. Some – men and women – have difficulty identifying with either gender and remain sexually neutral. Through this internal balance you're able to understand and appreciate the opposite sex and know what pleases them. You may even prefer their company to those of your own kind.

## The Naming Game

Some of your favourite phrases are 'What do you think?' and 'You would have really loved it/hated it'. You also tend to make liberal use of the names of the people you are talking to, to ensure that you attract their attention. Sometimes you can even wield names like weapons to disarm would-be opponents and protect yourself. Who can resist that half-playful, half-reproachful 'Now, John . . .' (or Alice or Robert or whoever)?

## Gentle Persuasion

Don't be fooled by all the courtesy and eagerness to please into thinking that Librans are pushovers. Those who underestimate the shrewdness of your tactics could be in for a big surprise. An iron fist fits snugly inside that elegant velvet glove, as those who have gone too far with a Libran have discovered to their cost. No one can force you to do what you don't want to do. Libra is a cardinal sign, which means you've always got some goal in mind – and often an eye for the main chance. You're generally cooperative but, translated, that can mean 'Let's do things my way!' Then, with dimpled smiles and never a raised voice, you'll use your considerable charms to manoeuvre others into doing exactly what you want. With your gift of getting your own way with the minimum of offence, you can even give people the impression that it was their idea in the first place. So everybody's happy.

## Flighty Flirts
Librans are born charmers and skilled at the arts of teasing and flirting. You know instinctively how to make a man or woman feel that they are the most interesting and desirable person in the room – and, in return, you love getting their undivided attention, together with that frisson of connectedness and unspoken possibilities. Who can resist your sweet nothings!? You're usually not serious about the games you play, as you'll flirt with everyone from children and dogs to little old ladies. For you, it's just part of civilised living, but some disapproving sobersides can find you frivolous and flighty.

## Mirror, Mirror . . .
As you identify so much with others, if anyone manages to resist your charms you'll try twice as hard to bring them under your spell. Some insecure Librans revel in the power they have to lure others and can play cruel games to boost their own egos and vanity. They'll lead on people in whom they have no interest, just to demonstrate how irresistibly attractive they are. Most dangerous of all is the killer bimbo (both male and female) who will target and deliberately lure away someone else's partner. Then, when the victim is hooked and head over heels in love, they'll withdraw abruptly and move on to the next potential trophy, leaving emotional devastation in their wake. All may be fair in love and war, but this is the department of dirty tricks and if you find yourself indulging in such behaviour, just think – is it fair, and how would you feel if it happened to you?

## Everything in Moderation

Like the Libran scales, your balance point is rarely static. You can swing between being frantically busy and energetic, then collapsing on the sofa, lethargic and lazy, peeling yourself grapes, or chocolate bars. You can be sweet and helpful one day then flip into all-out self-centredness the next. It's because you need moderation and the happy medium, not perfection, or extremes of any kind. Although you love peace, if things have been too nice and agreeable for too long you'll stir up an argument or controversy just to even up the score. A few Librans seem constantly to side with darkness and life's uglier views – think of the black magician Aleister Crowley, once called the wickedest man in the world. But even the devil needs an advocate. It's only fair, after all.

## Whose Side Are You On?

Ideas and principles fascinate Librans. As your head generally rules your heart, you'll rarely let emotions cloud your judgement. In conversation you tend to say 'I think' rather than 'I feel'. Debating is often your best way to learn, as you enjoy the to-ing and fro-ing, and arguing the pros and cons. You may not be particularly concerned what the discussion is about. It's the fun of interacting that counts. As you can keep a cool head in controversies, without getting heated up or emotionally entangled, it's sometimes hard for you to understand that there are others who can't. You can see advantages and disadvantages in every point of view and, if you think the opposite view isn't being properly represented, you may even switch sides mid-sentence, infuriating your allies and confusing opponents. This can make you seem frivolous or disloyal but it's more the case that prejudice, dogma, exaggerations or unfair accusations outrage your sense of proportion and, as a reflex reaction, you'll balance the argument with an opposing view. You know that half the truth is often a whole lie and would probably agree with Niels Bohr, the Libran physicist who developed quantum mechanics. He said that profound truths can be recognised by the fact that their opposite is also true. Other signs often don't get this.

## The Finer Things of Life

Beauty, elegance and culture are as necessary to you as food and drink. Most Librans have a refined appreciation of music, art and colour. Even if you're not conventionally beautiful, you're likely to have an air of graciousness about you. The way you dress and arrange your home and office reflects your strong sense of harmony. Harmony, one of Libra's key words, means fitting together like a joint, and that's your special talent – joining together people and objects and ideas in apt and pleasing relationships. You take pleasure in leaving every situation just that little bit better and more polished than it was before you arrived. You're a wonderful social organiser, as you know how to fuse wildly different personalities into a well-functioning group. One of nature's matchmakers, you love bringing people together, because when others are happy, you are happy, too.

## Money, Money, Money

The best things in life may be free for other signs, but rarely so for a Libran. Stylishness, elegance and sumptuousness can carry a hefty price tag and it's often a case of once seen, simply must have. However, with your chess player's ability to work out every move in advance, if you set your mind to it, you can be excellent at sensible financial planning and coming up with clever strategies for making money.

## Libra at Work

As you prefer to have a sounding board for decisions and ideas, working in partnership, rather than alone, often suits you best. You're a natural at steering group dynamics, persuading people to cooperate while sorting out disputes tactfully and ensuring nobody feels excluded. As a boss, you'll treat employees as equals and you expect your superiors to do the same to you. You will happily work *with* bosses but not for, or under, them. Some underhand Librans use their management skills slickly, to their own advantage. They'll set up their more aggressive opponents for a major dispute, then, having divided, will step in and rule, slipping themselves deftly into the position of power.

You're much more suited to mental, rather than menial, work. Dirt, disharmony and ugliness make you feel quite ill. So do unfriendly or uncooperative fellow employees and bosses who shout or order you around. You're great at getting the ball rolling on new projects and at encouraging other, less motivated people to fall in with your plans. You can be quite determined and, though it will rarely show, once you've made up your mind, you're not easily swayed by what other people want.

Your peculiar work rhythm needs to be respected. You'll work extremely hard for a while and then, suddenly and for no apparent reason, you'll flag and potter around, doing very little. There's no good trying to achieve much then. It simply won't happen. Then, out of the blue, you're raring to go again. It's just the Libran pendulum effect at work again.

## Ideal Careers

Your love of debate, passionate belief in fairness and human dignity, coupled with your ability to distance yourself from purely emotional considerations, makes a career in law an excellent choice. Conciliation and arbitration rather than litigation, and defence rather than prosecution, are usually your preferences and you have all the right qualities to make an impartial judge. For the same reasons, many Librans are to be found in trade unions, politics and the diplomatic service.

Successful chess players and generals often have Libra prominent. This helps them understand and anticipate their opponents' motives, position and tactics and plan accordingly, so winning the battle before the combat even starts. Other Librans favour the arts as musicians, painters, photographers and writers. Your eye for harmony is just what's needed in the world of beauty, textiles, fashion and interior design. Many top architects have Libra somewhere prominent in their birth charts. Anything that involves people-pleasing – personnel and reception work and customer relations – could also suit you.

Librans at work offer the best of both worlds. You're a decorative asset to any workplace: charming, well-groomed and immaculately dressed. And you've a fine brain to match the externals. There are probably more Libran female bosses than from any other sign, except Cancer and Capricorn.

## Libra and Health

Libra rules the kidneys, which maintain the correct balance of the body's water and chemicals. Venus, Libra's planet, rules the endocrine system, which, via hormones, keeps the body in the steady state that it needs to function.

You may be liable to cystitis and kidney and bladder problems, especially when your relationships are troubled. Indecision and trying to please everybody, while ignoring your own needs, can deplete your energy and may even lead to depression, headaches, skin rashes and eye problems. Attending to your own requirements could help to relieve your symptoms. Like Libran Oscar Wilde, you're probably able to 'resist everything except temptation', especially when it comes to luxury foods and fine wines. This, combined with your periodic phases of sofa slouching, can lead to the scales not always tipping in your favour. Self-discipline is probably not your strongest point, nor is sticking to a strict health regime. Looking at body care as pampering, rather than self-denial, is a far better tactic. Exercise that involves partners, like dancing, tennis and fencing, could appeal. Beautiful surroundings help keep you calm, as does massage, yoga and music.

## Libra Relating

Life, for Librans, *is* relationship. Too much solitude feels unnatural to you and the idea of growing old alone is not a happy one. Without a partner, either romantic, business or sparring, you feel incomplete. You usually function better when you're half of a twosome – it makes you feel stronger, and much more secure. Your deepest fear is to be abandoned, or betrayed, romantically. You tend to think in terms of 'we' rather than 'I', as you much prefer a shared experience to going solo. Librans believe passionately in equality and fair play, both at work and at home. Men with Libra strong in their charts are particularly good at shouldering their fair share of housework and child-care.

## Falling in Love with Love

You're romantic to the core and long to live out the perfect love story. When you're with a partner, you love to have all the right props – flowers, poetry, soft music, elegant surroundings, champagne and the gentle flicker of candlelight. The art of chivalry is alive and well and living in the hearts of Librans. You like to show and be shown admiration and appreciation, and all the elegant little gestures of courtesy and good manners are important to you. A partner who is your equal intellectually, as well as being physically, culturally and emotionally compatible, is what you long for.

## Fairy-tale Romance

As you dream of the perfect partner, one who could exist only in fairy tales, you are often disappointed by the flawed mere mortals that surround you. It's difficult for you to handle the cruder realities of life, most especially in relationships, and you can feel awkward around emotional intimacy, as you're more at home in the world of ideas and ideals. You're expert at rationalising away your own emotions and are often uncomfortable with those of other people, so you'd prefer a partner who isn't going to trample on your dreams or embarrass you with distasteful outbursts of anger or passion. Often you'll enjoy discussing feelings and what makes people behave the way they do, but don't really enjoy experiencing strong emotions. They can make you feel apprehensive and out of control.

You tend to idealise people you love and put them on a pedestal then admire them through relentlessly thick rose-tinted spectacles. Falling in love with love may be falling for make-believe, but you're determined to make the fantasy real. This may mean trying to change your partner to fit into the ideal you have in mind. Sadly, this can lead to real problems if your partner gets fed up of being manoeuvred into being somebody they're not. When you can see, accept and love your partner as he or she really is, then the authentic meeting of equal and interdependent souls that you long for can finally take place.

## The End of the Road

Disentangling yourself from a relationship that's come to an end is hard, as breaking up goes against everything in your nature. Because you hate and fear being on your own, you can be prepared to take crumbs rather than no cake at all. You can put off the final curtain until one day you'll lose patience and end it abruptly. More often, though, you'll try to manipulate the other person into breaking it off, rather than doing it yourself. Then they, and not you, get to be Ms or Mr Nasty.

## Libra and Sex

You often prefer your partner to make the first move and so can seem quite passive. In reality, though, you're the one giving out signals and subtly seducing your partner into taking the initiative – and thinking it was his or her idea. You find it difficult to say no if you're not in the mood, so more often than not you'll evade the issue with a 'Not tonight, darling' headache. To enjoy sex you need to have tasteful surroundings and plenty of time. Unless Scorpio is strong in your chart, anything sordid is a real turn-off for you. You have the delightful knack of making your partner feel that they're the world's greatest lover – and you're likely be highly skilled in the bedroom arts yourself.

# SIX

# Aspects of the Sun

PLANETS, JUST LIKE PEOPLE, CAN HAVE IMPORTANT RELATIONSHIPS with each other. These relationships are called aspects. Aspects to your Sun from any other planet can influence your personality markedly. The most powerful effects come with those from the slower-moving planets – Saturn, Uranus, Neptune or Pluto. Sometimes they can alter your ideas about yourself and your behaviour patterns so much that you may not feel at all typical of your sign in certain areas of your life.

Check if your birth date and year appear in the various sections below to find out if one or more of these planets was aspecting the Sun when you were born. Only the so-called challenging aspects have been included. These are formed when the planets are together, opposite or at right angles to each other in the sky.

Unfortunately, because space is restricted, other aspects have been left out, although they have similar effects to those described below and, for the same reason, a few dates will inevitably have been missed out, too. (You can find out for sure whether or not your Sun is aspected at my website

41

www.janeridderpatrick.com.) If your Sun has no aspects to
Saturn, Uranus, Neptune or Pluto, you're more likely to be
a typical Libran.

Some well-known Librans with challenging aspects to
their Suns appear below. You can find more in the birthday
section at the end of the book.

## Sun in Libra in Aspect with Saturn

If you were born between 1951 and 1953 and 1980 and
1982, whether or not your birthday is listed below, you are
likely to feel the influence of Saturn on your Sun.

23 September–3 October in: 1930, 1937–8, 1944, 1951, 1959–60,
1967, 1973, 1980–81, 1988–9 and 1996
4–13 October in: 1931, 1938, 1944, 1952, 1960, 1967, 1974, 1981,
1990, 1997
14–23 October in: 1932, 1939, 1952–3, 1961, 1968, 1975, 1982,
1990–91, 1998

| | | |
|---|---|---|
| Terence Conran | Bob Geldof | Deborah Kerr |
| Vladimir Putin | Anne Robinson | Serena Williams |

You could have a bit of an ambivalent attitude to authority.
On the one hand, you have a powerful, though sometimes
carefully concealed, ambition to be top of the pile yourself.
On the other hand, because the part of you that feels
inadequate expects to be found out, and taken to task for
wrong-doing, you could, quite unconsciously, set yourself
up to behave in a way that's almost calculated to bring you
the disapproval you fear so much. It doesn't have to be like
this. It is possible that in childhood you had some
humiliating experiences of you, or your father, being
overlooked, put down or shamed for not living up to
somebody else's expectations. If you still believe, as an

adult, that you are a victim of some authority figure 'out there' who is judging you and holding you back, you can be stubbornly uncooperative and oversensitive to criticism, or even turn into someone who dishes out criticism or punishment yourself.

Your challenge in life is to embody the principles of harmony, justice, fair play – or, like Terence Conran, elegant design – and to take on the responsibility to ensure that they are upheld. The more you push yourself forward without considering others, the harder you could fall from time to time. Coming to terms with life's limitations will pay off. Wherever Saturn is around, you have to work your passage and expect a few learning experiences en route. By accepting those conditions with grace, you are well on your way to the top. You'll only be truly happy when you stop seeking approval from others, set your own goals and put all your efforts into attaining them fairly. Nothing stands in the way of your success except your own fear of failure.

## Sun in Libra in Aspect with Uranus
If you were born between 1968 and 1974, whether or not your birthday is listed below, you are likely to feel the influence of Uranus on your Sun.

23 September–3 October in: 1947–51, 1968–71 and 1988–91
4–13 October in: 1929–32, 1950–53, 1970–73, 1991–94
14–23 October in: 1931–4, 1952–6, 1972–5 and 1993–96

| | | |
|---|---|---|
| Annie Besant | Betty Boothroyd | Michael Collins |
| Lord Alfred Douglas | Eminem | Carrie Fisher |

Uranus, planet of reform and rebellion, creates life's trailblazers, eccentrics and outsiders, as well as some of our most brilliant innovators, social activists and reformers.

Whatever else you are, you're certainly not dull. Your career and relationships are likely to be unusual in some way, and you're unlikely to bow down quietly to convention. The election of Betty Boothroyd, a much-respected former Speaker of the House of Commons, was remarkable in several ways. It was the first time a Speaker had been elected from the opposition benches for over 150 years, and a tradition of six centuries was broken by electing a woman – and one who had been a chorus girl before going into politics. From being a Labour Party activist, she shifted to a role of complete Libran impartiality. As she said. 'It's my duty. Nothing else will do.'

Sometimes being out on a limb is uncomfortable and dangerous, as Lord Alfred Douglas, lover of Oscar Wilde, found to his cost. Simply because he was outed as gay at a time when that was socially unacceptable, he ended up imprisoned and outcast. What often seems odd or outrageous when you do it, simply because it's new, is more than likely to be part of mainstream thinking a few years down the line. You need a constant diet of new experiences and challenges to work on, or you'll quickly become bored. You could be a brilliant strategist, but once you've achieved your objectives you're liable to become restless; be careful not to sabotage your own good work and success by uprooting yourself and moving on too abruptly. Your father may have been unusual in some way and a conventional partnership may not always suit you because you do need so much freedom.

## Sun in Libra in Aspect with Neptune

If you were born between 1942 and 56, whether or not your birthday is listed below, you are likely to feel the influence of Neptune on your Sun.

23 September–3 October in: 1941–9 and 1988–92
4–13 October in: 1947–54 and 1989–95
14–23 October in: 1952–9 and 1992–9

| Mahatma Gandhi | Bob Geldof | Felicity Kendal |
| Linda McCartney | Alfred Nobel | Ann Widdecombe |

Neptune heightens your sensitivity to beauty and harmony, as well as to suffering, and you could find ugliness or conflict quite unbearable. Yet your Libra Sun hates injustice and you'll feel guilty unless you act as an advocate for the oppressed or deprived. Bob Geldof was so moved by pictures of millions starving in Ethiopia that he badgered big-name pop stars to produce 'Do They Know It's Christmas?' which became the fastest-selling single ever recorded. He then organised the huge Band Aid concert which raised another £40 million for famine relief. Alfred Nobel, the inventor of dynamite, was a committed pacifist who amassed a great fortune. He left the bulk of his wealth to create prestigious international awards, including the Nobel Peace Prize.

You may have vague feelings of helplessness, guilt or unworthiness and could become heavily dependent on your partner for confidence and protection. Gandhi was always filled with self-doubt and, as a child, was so timid that he rarely spoke to anyone. Yet he rose above his shyness to become the champion of the Indian people, despite terrible hardships and opposition.

You may be drawn to mysticism or spirituality and work to develop the highest qualities in yourself and others. Other people may see you as a glamorous icon, but if you start to believe the fantasies about yourself you are in deep trouble. You may idealise your father, but feel that he is somehow just out of reach, or that he is more accessible to others than to you. You also need to learn to say no – firmly – as you tend to take on too much trying to help others. Do be careful, too, if life gets tough, of using the escape routes of alcohol or food, as you could be susceptible to allergies and addictions and piling on the pounds. Music and meditation are much better options.

## Sun in Libra in Aspect with Pluto

If you were born between 1971 and 1983, whether or not your birthday is listed below, you are likely to feel the influence of Pluto on your Sun.

23 September–3 October in: 1970–7
4–13 October in: 1975–81
14–23 October in: 1930–39 and 1979–1985

| | | |
|---|---|---|
| Richard Harris | Catherine Zeta Jones | Friedrich Nietzsche |
| Pelé | Margaret Thatcher | Kate Winslet |

Pluto, planet of survival and transformation, usually ensures that power, death, secrets or wealth will touch your life one way or another. Either you will be the one wielding the power, or you may at some time experience it being used against you. Your life can be divided into quite distinct stages, where you leave the past behind forever and have to reinvent yourself. Pelé rose from a childhood of poverty to become one of the finest footballers ever. So great was his reputation that Nigeria halted a war for 48 hours so that he could play there. Yet, despite his success, massive debts drove him back to the game after his retirement. Most with this aspect refuse to tolerate corruption, hypocrisy or bullying, and will not rest until they've exposed the culprits and rooted them out. Others can be a bit dictatorial themselves, and believe that attack is the best form of defence. Be careful, though, not to come on too strong; some people could mistake it for intimidation and be tempted to retaliate.

Others are drawn into the darker, more taboo areas of life, like sex, violence or drug abuse. Nietzsche, who wrote 'What does not destroy me makes me stronger', believed in 'the will to power'. He died, insane, from syphilis. His philosophy was later borrowed and perverted by the Nazis in their own pursuit of power. Your will and determination are formidable; combined with your ability to plan like a chess player, when you set your mind on a course of action nobody and nothing is going to be allowed to stand in your way. The lady (or man) is not for turning! You can go against the odds and into extreme conditions to achieve success. Peace comes when you stop trying to control the world and learn to trust the life process itself.

# SEVEN

# Meeting Your Moon

☽ THE GLYPH FOR THE MOON IS THE SEMI-CIRCLE OR CRESCENT. It is a symbol for the receptiveness of the soul and is associated with feminine energies and the ebb and flow of the rhythms of life. In some Islamic traditions it represents the gateway to paradise and the realms of bliss.

The Sun and Moon are the two complementary poles of your personality, like yang and yin, masculine and feminine, active and reflective, career and home, father and mother. The Moon comes into its own as a guide at night, the time of sleeping consciousness. It also has a powerful effect on the waters of the earth. Likewise, the Moon in your birth chart describes what you respond to instinctively and feel 'in your waters', often just below the level of consciousness. It is your private radar system, sending you messages via your body responses and feelings, telling you whether a situation seems safe or scary, nice or nasty. Feelings provide vital information about circumstances in and around you. Ignore them at your peril; that will lead you into emotional, and sometimes even physical, danger. Eating disorders tend to be associated with being out of touch with, or neglecting, the instincts and the body, both of which the Moon describes.

Extraordinary though it might seem to those who are emotionally tuned in, some people have great difficulty in knowing what they are feeling. One simple way is to pay attention to your body. Notice any sensations that attract your attention. Those are linked to your feelings. Now get a sense of whether they are pleasant or unpleasant, then try to put a more exact name to what those feelings might be. Is it sadness, happiness, fear? What is it that they are trying to tell you? Your Moon hints at what will strongly activate your feelings. Learning to trust and decode this information will help make the world seem — and be — a safer place.

The Moon represents your drive to nurture and protect yourself and others. Its sign, house and aspects describe how you respond and adapt emotionally to situations and what feeds you, in every sense of the word. It gives information about your home and home life and how you experienced your mother, family and childhood, as well as describing your comfort zone of what feels familiar — the words 'family' and 'familiar' come from the same source. It shows, too, what makes you feel secure and what could comfort you when you're feeling anxious. Your Moon describes what moves and motivates you powerfully at the deepest instinctual level and indicates what is truly the 'matter' in — or with — your life.

Knowing children's Moon signs can help parents and teachers better understand their insecurities and respect their emotional make-up and needs, and so prevent unnecessary hurt, or even harm, to sensitive young lives. It's all too easy to expect that our children and parents should have the same emotional wiring as we do, but that's rarely how life works. Finding our parents' Moon signs can be a real revelation. It can often help us understand where they are coming from, what they need and why they react to us in the way they do. Many of my clients have been able to find the understanding and compassion to forgive their parents when they realised that they were doing their very best with the emotional resources available to them.

In relationships it is important that your Moon's requirements are met to a good enough extent. For example, if you have your Moon in Sagittarius you must have adventure, freedom and the opportunity to express your beliefs. If being with your partner constantly violates these basic needs, you will never feel secure and loved and the relationship could, in the long term, undermine you. However, if your Moon feels too comfortable, you will never change and grow. The art is to get a good working balance between support and challenge.

A man's Moon sign can show some of the qualities he will unconsciously select in a wife or partner. Some of the others are shown in his Venus sign. Many women can seem much more like their Moon signs than their Sun signs, especially if they are involved in mothering a family and being a support system for their husbands or partners. It is only at the mid-life crisis that many women start to identify more with the qualities of their own Suns rather than living that out through their partners' ambitions. Similarly, men tend to live out the characteristics of their Moon signs through their wives and partners until mid-life, often quite cut off from their own feelings and emotional responses. If a man doesn't seem at all like his Moon sign, then check out the women in his life. There's a good chance that his wife, mother or daughter will show these qualities.

Your Moon can be in any sign, including the same one as your Sun. Each sign belongs to one of the four elements: Fire, Earth, Air or Water. The element of your Moon can give you a general idea of how you respond to new situations and what you need to feel safe and comforted. We all become anxious if our Moon's needs are not being recognised and attended to. We then, automatically, go into our personal little rituals for making ourselves feel better. Whenever you are feeling distressed, especially when you are way out of your comfort zone in an unfamiliar situation, do something to feed and soothe your Moon. You're almost certain to calm down quickly.

## Fire Moons

If you have a fire Moon in Aries, Leo or Sagittarius, your first response to any situation is to investigate in your imagination the possibilities for drama, excitement and self-expression. Feeling trapped by dreary routine in an ordinary humdrum life crushes you completely. Knowing that you are carrying out a special mission feeds your soul. To you, all the world's a stage and a voyage of discovery. Unless you are at the centre of the action playing some meaningful role, anxiety and depression can set in. To feel secure, you have to have an appropriate outlet for expressing your spontaneity, honourable instincts and passionate need to be of unique significance. The acknowledgement, appreciation and feedback of people around you are essential, or you don't feel real. Not to be seen and appreciated, or to be overlooked, can feel like a threat to your very existence.

## Earth Moons

If you have an earth Moon in Taurus, Virgo or Capricorn, you'll respond to new situations cautiously and practically. Rapidly changing circumstances where you feel swept along and out of control are hard for you to cope with. You need time for impressions to sink in. Sometimes it is only much later, after an event has taken place, that you become sure what you felt about it. Your security lies in slowing down, following familiar routines and rituals, even if they are a bit obsessive, and focusing on something, preferably material – possibly the body itself or nature – which is comforting because it is still there. Indulging the senses in some way often helps too, through food, sex or body care. So does taking charge of the practicalities of the immediate situation, even if this is only mixing the drinks or passing out clipboards. To feel secure, you need continuity and a sense that you have your hand on the rudder of your own life. Think of the rather irreverent joke about the man seeming to cross himself in a crisis, all the while actually touching his most valued possessions to check that they are still intact – spectacles, testicles, wallet and watch. That must have been thought up by someone with the Moon in an earth sign.

## Air Moons

When your Moon is in an air sign – Gemini, Libra or Aquarius – you feel most secure when you can stand back from situations and observe them from a distance. Too much intimacy chokes you and you'll tend to escape it by going into your head to the safety of ideas and analysis. Even in close relationships you need your mental, and preferably physical, space. You often have to think, talk or write about what you are feeling before you are sure what your feelings are. By putting them 'out there' so that you can examine them clearly, you can claim them as your own. Unfairness and unethical behaviour can upset you badly and make you feel uneasy until you have done something about it or responded in some way. It can be easy with an air Moon to be unaware of, or to ignore, your own feelings because you are more responsive to ideas, people and situations outside of yourself that may seem to have little connection with you. This is not a good idea, as it cuts you off from the needs of your body as well as your own emotional intelligence. Making opportunities to talk, play with and exchange ideas and information can reduce the stress levels if anxiety strikes.

## Water Moons

Finally, if your Moon is in a water sign – Cancer, Scorpio or Pisces – you are ultra-sensitive to atmospheres, and you can experience other people's pain or distress as if they were your own. You tend to take everything personally and, even if the situation has nothing at all to do with you, feel responsible for making it better. Your worst nightmare is to feel no emotional response coming back from other people. That activates your deep-seated terror of abandonment, which can make you feel that you don't exist and is, quite literally, what you fear even more than death. If you feel insecure, you may be tempted to resort to emotional manipulation to try to force intimacy with others – not a good idea, as this can lead to the very rejection that you dread. You are at your most secure when the emotional climate is positive and you have trusted, supportive folk around who will winkle you out of hiding if you become too reclusive. With a water Moon, it is vital to learn to value your own feelings and to take them seriously – and to have a safe, private place you can retreat to when you feel emotionally fragile. As you never forget anything which has made a feeling impression on you, sometimes your reactions are triggered by unconscious memories of things long past, rather than what is taking place in the present. When you learn to interpret them correctly, your feelings are your finest ally and will serve you well.

## Finding Your Moon Sign

If you don't yet know your Moon sign, before looking it up, you could have some fun reading through the descriptions that follow and seeing if you can guess which one it is. To find your Moon sign, check your year and date of birth in the tables on pp. 99–112. For a greater in-depth understanding of your Moon sign, you might like to read about its characteristics in the book in this series about that sign.

At the beginning of each section are the names of some well-known Librans with that particular Moon sign. You can find more about them in Chapter Ten.

## Sun in Libra with Moon in Aries

| | | |
|---|---|---|
| Marc Bolan | Miguel de Cervantes | Heinrich Himmler |
| Luciano Pavarotti | Anita Roddick | Sarah Ferguson, Duchess of York |

An Aries Moon means that action, in one form or another, is essential in your life. At its best you can be involved in tough, competitive or pioneering enterprises that are linked with partnerships with others. Anita Roddick, who founded the Body Shop, has managed to create from scratch a successful business empire that combines the principles of social and environmental justice with profitability. She personally makes frequent pioneering expeditions abroad to discover new ingredients for products.

Part of you hates confrontation, but you've a knack of stirring up conflict or controversy wherever you go, unless you find a suitable outlet for your spontaneous combustibility. Impulsive and daring, you live for the moment and often forget to reflect on the consequences of rash words and actions until they have been said and done. Like Cervantes' chivalry-seeking hero, Don Quixote, you leap to the defence of the helpless and would love to destroy the wicked. However, like Quixote, who charged at windmills mistaking them for giants, you can be so quick off the draw that you too may sometimes charge, head-down and ignoring cautionary advice, at inappropriate targets. Fun-loving Sarah Ferguson, former wife of Prince Andrew, was constantly in hot water for acting exuberantly on the spur of the moment and forgetting royal protocol. Occasionally, Aries equals violence, either as victim or perpetrator. Fortunately, those with this combination rarely choose to be as brutal as Nazi leader Heinrich Himmler, whose plans were responsible for the deaths of millions. Aries and accidents are often linked. If those do happen, it's almost certainly time to slow down, pull back and check whether you're channelling all of your dynamic energy in the right direction

## Sun in Libra with Moon in Taurus

| F. Scott Fitzgerald | Elinor Glyn | Jesse Jackson |
| Harold Pinter | Peter Stringfellow | Anne Widdecombe |

When in need of comfort you'll automatically reach out for sensual pleasures like food or sex or plain old-fashioned shopping therapy. Your physical appetites are large and in some this can mean a powerful libido and a reluctance to restrict themselves to just one partner. Peter Stringfellow, the nightclub owner, claims to have slept with over 2,000 women and is, reportedly, still notching bedposts. Writer of racy fiction Elinor Glyn inspired the following anonymous verse: 'Would you like to sin, With Elinor Glyn, On a tiger skin? Or would you prefer, To err, with her, On some other fur?'

You need not, however, be dominated by your sexual passions. As you are idealistic about relationships, divorce or breaking up is a major trauma, so it's more than likely you wouldn't risk endangering a settled relationship. As material security is vitally important, having enough money is top priority. If your bank balance sinks below a certain level, you'll start to feel jittery. Fortunately, you are well-equipped with tactics for ensuring that the wolf stays well away from your door.

For peace of mind, you need to feel in control and to have a sense of ongoing safety, security and stability, so you like law and order to prevail. Many with this mix are drawn to politics, or the legal profession, for just that reason. Firmness of resolve is your virtue, but an occasional check that this hasn't congealed into inflexibility wouldn't go amiss. It's a rare person with a Moon in Taurus who doesn't enjoy music and art. Too long between mealtimes can make you irritable, as you need regular refuelling – and for you, a beautiful, peaceful place to retreat, preferably with a garden, is a necessity, not a luxury.

## Sun in Libra with Moon in Gemini

| Brigitte Bardot | Geoffrey Boycott | Edwina Currie |
|---|---|---|
| T.S. Eliot | Groucho Marx | Roger Moore |

With your low boredom threshold and powerful curiosity, you can be distracted momentarily by just about everything, or anyone, that crosses your path. Skill with words is your speciality. Groucho Marx wrote to a club, resigning, saying that he wouldn't want to join a club that would have him as a member. You aren't above borrowing the ideas of others either. According to T.S. Eliot, 'Immature poets imitate; mature poets steal.' Spin doctors could learn a thing or two from you, as you are adept at lightning-quick analyses, lateral thinking and putting two and two together to come up with brilliant and often simple solutions to both theoretical and practical problems. You can use your clever tongue to talk your way into, or out of, tricky situations. Not being allowed to communicate, share and comment on your experiences is like being starved of oxygen.

You could be a bit of a flirt and a thorough charmer. With your cheeky wit and way with words, you're unlikely to find much difficulty in coaxing others to fall in with your plans. You make an excellent reporter, commentator, writer and mimic, as you are quick to pick up the essence of what is going on and pass it on with a few deft phrases. Often you only know what your feelings are by talking or writing about them. You need frequent change to keep your mind fed with fresh ideas and it's not easy for you to concentrate your energies on just one person, career or project. Travelling refreshes you and with your love of freedom you can't bear to be tied down to too much routine. Being constantly on the move is more your style.

## Sun in Libra with Moon in Cancer

| Annie Besant | Melvyn Bragg | Graham Greene |
| Eleanor Roosevelt | Paul Simon | P.G. Wodehouse |

Being highly intuitive, you can quickly pick up on atmospheres and tune in to the feelings of those around, giving you an instant rapport with others. It's all too easy for you to interpret other people's withdrawals and sulks as personal snubs when they may actually have nothing to do with you at all. As you are terrified of humiliation and rejection, this can make you withdraw emotionally as self-protection.

You hate confrontation every bit as much as you dislike examining your feelings, so, unless you find some outlet for your emotional build-up, it's easy to become resentful without even realising it, until you either explode or burst into tears. Man or woman, you have a powerful mothering instinct and you may enjoy feeding loved ones or, like Paul Simon, building a 'bridge over troubled waters'. Graham Greene gave financial help to several struggling writers, often sending along a few comforting bottles of wine, too, just for good measure. Your need to care for others, and passion for justice may be expressed in campaigning work like that of Annie Besant and Eleanor Roosevelt, who did much to improve social and working conditions for women.

What is familiar is what feels safe. Family matters to you and you are gentle, kind and helpful to anyone in need. You need warm, secure and intimate relationships which, once established, could last forever. It's important to be careful with whom you associate, as you need to give and receive tenderness and protection. With your reclusive tendency, you may enjoy creating a warm, cosy nest where you can plump up the pillows and curl up in bed with a hot, comforting drink and retreat from the outside world.

## Sun in Libra with Moon in Leo

| | | |
|---|---|---|
| Catherine Deneuve | Mahatma Gandhi | Mark Hamill |
| Dr Samuel Johnson | Margaret Thatcher | Oscar Wilde |

You urgently need an honourable role to play, where it is

appropriate for you to stand in the spotlight, radiating generosity, leadership and integrity. Your challenge is to make sure that the role you take on brings out the best and not the worst of Leo traits (pomposity, snootiness and self-absorption), as you have so much to give. The film role of Luke Skywalker that Mark Hamill played in the *Star Wars* trilogy shows your combination working beautifully. More than likely you're a natural leader, with formidable organising skills. Some with this combination can be somewhat bossy and domineering in their unquestioning belief in their right to be in charge. You've a knack, however, of getting your own way and with your natural charm, charisma and regal bearing, one smile from you and any opposition to your plans usually melts away like snow on a sunny day. Some in Margaret Thatcher's government were half in love with her.

Ambition and self-promotion usually come easily to you. Confidence and pizzazz ooze out of every pore and it would rarely occur to you that you might be wrong. Oscar Wilde was asked by customs on entering America whether he had anything to declare. 'Only my genius,' he replied. In the quiet of your own heart, though, you may sometimes pause for self-reflection. Indian leader Mahatma Gandhi struggled long and hard to subdue his vanity. Others with this combination scarcely seem to give the matter much thought. There's part of you that adores getting dressed up, socialising with the crème de la crème and being made a fuss of. You expect the finest and usually get it. When every eye is turned on you, and you are looking your best, then all's well in your world.

## Sun in Libra with Moon in Virgo

| | | |
|---|---|---|
| Deepak Chopra | Jean-Claude van Damme | Deborah Kerr |
| Aimee Semple McPherson | Serena Williams | Horatio, Lord Nelson |

Being of service keeps you grounded, but you do like to do things your way. When Admiral Nelson, during a naval battle, was flagged to cease action, he put a telescope to his blind eye and claimed he couldn't see the signal – then fought on to victory. You don't care much for slackers. You'll have your own version of Nelson's stirring statement 'England expects that every man will do his duty' which often brings out the best in others.

With your ability to spot flaws, and a first-class capacity for planning and organisation, you can be a gifted problem-solver, coming up with just the right solution that others had overlooked. In business, you are well-suited to administrative or executive positions. In creative fields, you make a skilled artist and craftsperson, going to endless trouble to ensure that the finished article is both elegant and useful. You like to know how things work and be able to operate them yourself. Depending on your interests, these may be social niceties, systems of thinking or mechanical contraptions. But whatever they are, you're likely to end up an expert. Healthcare, too, often interests you.

Orderly rituals, even simple ones like untangling your paperclips or squeezing your breakfast oranges slowly, can be immensely comforting in times of stress. Unfortunately, when you feel insecure you may be tempted to work even harder and end up with nerves all frazzled. You've a highly-strung nervous system, so quiet time alone for reflection is essential.

There is part of you that can hanker, nun-like, after the innocent purity of a simple life. Refinement and simplicity suit you, so cutting down to essentials and dejunking your life could be a perfect tonic from time to time.

## Sun in Libra with Moon in Libra

| Niels Bohr | Donna Karan | Doris Lessing |
| Bruce Springsteen | Sting | Kate Winslet |

Equality, fairness and harmony, or their lack, in relationships of all kinds – personal, political and material – are major themes of your life. Doris Lessing's *The Golden Notebook* explores the destructive relationships between men and women that mirror the disharmonies of materialistic societies. In his coat of arms the physicist Niels Bohr put, above the yin/yang symbols, the words 'opposites complement each other'. He devoted much of his later life to the peaceful application of atomic physics and to political problems caused by the development of atomic weapons.

Without a partner to bounce ideas off, you can feel at a bit of a loss. Unless Pluto or Scorpio features powerfully in your chart, coming up against the darker side of human nature could be a nasty shock, as you are deeply romantic and idealistic. It's often difficult for you to grasp the fact that some people are just not as nice and principled as you aim to be, and it can take a few hard knocks to shake you out of your ivory tower.

Unfairness and ugliness distress you, and you'll put considerable energy into righting, or fighting, what you feel is wrong. The singer Sting, with his wife and a Brazilian indian, started the Rainforest Foundation to help save the rainforests. Your distaste for anger and confrontation, as well as a preference for avoiding unpleasant feelings – your own as well as others' – can prevent you from sticking up for yourself even when it's appropriate. Being so altruistic and intent on justice for others, it's easy for you to overlook your own needs, but every so often the pendulum will swing the other way and you could let rip about how unfairly life is treating you.

## Sun in Libra with Moon in Scorpio

| | | |
|---|---|---|
| Julie Andrews | Jimmy Carter | Baroness Orczy |
| Will Smith | Midge Ure | Irvine Welsh |

Your feel intensely, and as a child you would have been acutely aware of any emotional, political or sexual undercurrents, bullying, coercion or secrets that weren't to be talked about in your family and community. You may even have felt that there was something unacceptable about you, or them, which could have left you with a sense of having to watch your back for potential nameless threats. If you've been hurt, you may be tempted to turn cynical and destructive but your greatest challenge is to refuse to be a victim of the past, and use your formidable willpower, insight and honesty to create a better and more authentic future for everyone, including yourself. As you can identify with them, you are acutely sensitive to people whose survival is threatened and may feel drawn to help them. Jimmy Carter, the former US president, set up a centre to wage peace, safeguard human rights and to alleviate suffering by eradicating its root causes. Ultravox singer Midge Ure was, with Bob Geldof, the driving force behind Band Aid in support of famine relief.

Underneath your calm, unruffled exterior is a simmering cauldron of powerful emotions that you'll prefer to keep strictly private. You have awesome reserves of emotional strength that come to your aid when your back is to the wall. Behind Julie Andrews' sweet, Mary Poppins image is a woman who has courageously come through much suffering and can still turn a smiling face to the world. You are first-class in business and politics, as you work well with others and, being highly intuitive, can smell a rat a mile off, so are unlikely to have the wool pulled over your eyes for long.

## Sun in Libra with Moon in Sagittarius

| | | |
|---|---|---|
| Ramsay MacDonald | Betty Boothroyd | Alyn Kirk |
| Queen Salawa | Friedrich Nietzsche | Christopher |
| Abeni | | Reeve |

Fair-minded and altruistic, many with this combination are drawn to politics and philosophy and are people on a mission. A born rover and idealist, too, in love with the adventure of life, you're constantly widening your horizons and going beyond the known and limiting, whether that means exploring foreign parts or stretching yourself mentally. You hate to be tied down, either by everyday responsibilities, or by the restrictions of the body. It's interesting that two of the actors who played Superman, Alyn Kirk and Christopher Reeve, as well as Friedrich Nietzsche, who developed the philosophy of the superman, all have this combination. Alternating depression and elation can dog a Sagittarius Moon, as it's hard to accept the limitations of being merely human. Happily, your faith in life and your own capabilities can become a self-fulfilling prophecy. Christopher Reeve, paralysed from the neck down after a riding accident, has already achieved the 'impossible' by moving a muscle.

Once you've got hold of a belief – or it's taken possession of you – there's little that will hold you back from trying to pass it on. Being both a perpetual student and a life-long teacher – and often preacher – giving advice comes as easily as breathing. Your passionate delivery can be inspiring, encouraging others to reach for the stars. This is a highly idealistic coupling, but you're usually smart enough not to mount the moral high ground too often as this can antagonise potential converts. You're a wonderful promoter and entrepreneur, trusting your hunches and happy to chance your luck. You need a partner who can share your enthusiasms and will give you plenty of freedom. The worst thing that could happen to you is to be tied down and not be allowed out to play.

## Sun in Libra with Moon in Capricorn

| | | |
|---|---|---|
| Matt Damon | Michael Douglas | Jim Henson |
| Lee Harvey Oswald | Anne Robinson | Jennifer Rush |

Highly ambitious and more than likely a workaholic, you will put your considerable determination into achieving your goals and making sure that you acquire the status and respect you crave. Many with this combination have come from humble backgrounds and work their way steadily to the top. Others were raised in homes where correct behaviour and discipline were the rule – rather than spontaneity and warm acceptance – or experienced some kind of emotional deprivation. This may have left you with a belief that it's only by working hard and pleasing the powers-that-be that you have a right to exist. You could be harsh with others you see as slackers or weak. Anne Robinson parodied this in her role as the dominatrix Queen of Mean quiz mistress in TV's *The Weakest Link*. It can be hard for you to express, or even pay attention to, your own emotional and physical needs but they don't go away just because you ignore them. Jim Henson, creator of the Muppets, didn't want to bother anyone about his feverish cold and ended up dying – unnecessarily, according to doctors – of pneumonia.

You are well able to look after yourself but you may cut yourself off from others by being so coolly independent. Unless you give in to the periodic depression that could plague you, you're headed straight up the ladder of success. You make a loyal and responsible partner if you can resist the temptation to put your home life in second place to your career or sense of duty. Oddly, solitude and sinking into melancholy feed you, so it is important to allow yourself to indulge in them from time to time, as well as taking time off to enjoy the rewards of your considerable labours.

## Sun in Libra with Moon in Aquarius

| Eminem | R.D. Laing | Timothy Leary |
|--------|-----------|---------------|
| John Lennon | Katherine Mansfield | Arthur Miller |

Because an Aquarius Moon is more tuned in to the changing needs of the community at large, rather than your own personal requirements, you could have a difficult relationship with your body, sometimes even forgetting to feed and care for it properly. It's often only when it protests by going on strike that you'll give it some attention. There can be a sizeable gap between your ideals and expectations of how society should function, and the reality of how it is. You find repugnant anything you classify as selfishness or emotional wallowing. Intimacy doesn't always come naturally and at times you may appear aloof and out of touch.

Your childhood may have been unusual or disrupted, or your mother cool, detached and independent – perhaps eccentric or ahead of her time. Even if you have lived in the same place all your life, you may feel like a displaced person, just waiting to be moved on. This can stop you putting down emotional roots anywhere and could lead to relationship tensions. Your challenge is to find some suitable alternative to the so-called 'normal' nuclear family. The controversial psychiatrist R.D. Laing found his by setting up a therapeutic community where staff and patients often changed places.

With your strong social conscience, injustice in society disturbs you and being involved with groups of like-minded people, who aim to make the world a better place and give peace a chance, soothes and supports you. Sometimes you feel more related to these people than your own biological family. You're at your most comfortable when you know that you are involved in reforming or rebelling against outworn attitudes, and you may even enjoy making a few shock waves yourself.

## Sun in Libra with Moon in Pisces

| | | |
|---|---|---|
| Chris de Burgh | Chubby Checker | Diana Dors |
| Rita Hayworth | Catherine Zeta Jones | Marie Stopes |

Your are an idealist and a dreamer longing to lose yourself in seamless bliss. Escaping from everyday reality at frequent intervals is essential for your well-being – though preferably not through the vehicle of alcohol or food, as this can get out of hand. Meditation, reading, films or music could suit you better. For some Librans, the sensitivity and dependency of this Moon can be unbearable and they erect a barrier of cynicism and aloofness to shut out their own vulnerable feelings.

As you absorb atmospheres like a sponge, you can't help but empathise with other people's pain, noticing especially if someone is suffering or expects something from you. You'll then feel guilty and edgy until you have complied with their unspoken plea, as your distress doesn't end until theirs does. As a child, you may have felt responsible for looking after your mother, who may not always have seemed available for you, and learned to read emotional atmospheres to get your own needs met indirectly. Celebrities with Pisces Moons can tune in to, and provide, the fantasy their audiences long for, like Chris de Burgh with his meltingly romantic 'Lady in Red'.

Beauty and poetry are food for your soul but when it comes to homemaking, muddle and mess, literally or metaphorically, may sometimes be more the disorder of the day. You need to be careful whom you allow into your personal space, as you can easily be sucked in to other people's realities and be pushed around or manipulated by stronger personalities. It's essential that you steer well clear of selfish partners as, hating confrontation, you may be too ready to compromise your own needs to accommodate the desires of others. A mutually supportive relationship is what's best for you, and what you deserve.

# EIGHT

# Mercury – It's All in the Mind

THE GLYPHS FOR THE PLANETS ARE MADE UP OF THREE SYMBOLS: the circle, the semi-circle and the cross. Mercury is the only planet, apart from Pluto, whose glyph is made up of all three of these symbols. At the bottom there is the cross, representing the material world; at the top is the semi-circle of the crescent Moon, symbolising the personal soul; and in the middle, linking these two, is the circle of eternity, expressed through the individual. In mythology, Mercury was the only god who had access to all three worlds – the underworld, the middle world of earth and the higher world of the gods. Mercury in your chart represents your ability, through your thoughts and words, to make connections between the inner world of your mind and emotions, the outer world of other people and events, and the higher world of intuition. Your Mercury sign can give you a great deal of information about the way your mind works and about your interests, communication skills and your preferred learning style.

It can be frustrating when we just can't get through to some people and it's easy to dismiss them as being either completely thick or deliberately obstructive. Chances are they are neither. It may be that you're simply not talking each other's languages. Knowing your own and other people's communication styles can lead to major breakthroughs in relationships.

Information about children's natural learning patterns can help us teach them more effectively. It's impossible to learn properly if the material isn't presented in a way that resonates with the way your mind works. You just can't 'hear' it, pick it up or grasp it. Wires then get crossed and the data simply isn't processed. Many children are seriously disadvantaged if learning materials and environments don't speak to them. You may even have been a child like that yourself. If so, you could easily have been left with the false impression that you are a poor learner just because you couldn't get a handle on the lessons being taught. Identifying your own learning style can be like finding the hidden key to the treasure room of knowledge.

The signs of the zodiac are divided into four groups by element:

> The fire signs: Aries, Leo and Sagittarius
> The earth signs: Taurus, Virgo and Capricorn
> The air signs: Gemini, Libra and Aquarius
> The water signs: Cancer, Scorpio and Pisces

Your Mercury will therefore belong to one of the four elements, depending on which sign it is in. Your Mercury can only be in one of three signs – the same sign as your Sun, the one before or the one after. This means that each sign has one learning style that is never natural to it. For Libra, this is the fire style.

Mercury in each of the elements has a distinctive way of

operating. I've given the following names to the learning and communicating styles of Mercury through the elements. Mercury in fire – active imaginative; Mercury in earth – practical; Mercury in air – logical; and Mercury in water – impressionable.

## Mercury in Fire: Active Imaginative

Your mind is wide open to the excitement of fresh ideas. It responds to action and to the creative possibilities of new situations. Drama, games and storytelling are excellent ways for you to learn. You love to have fun and play with ideas. Any material to be learned has to have some significance for you personally, or add to your self-esteem, otherwise you rapidly lose interest. You learn by acting out the new information, either physically or in your imagination. The most efficient way of succeeding in any goal is to make first a mental picture of your having achieved it. This is called mental rehearsal and is used by many top sportsmen and women as a technique to help improve their performance. You do this spontaneously, as your imagination is your greatest mental asset. You can run through future scenarios in your mind's eye and see, instantly, where a particular piece of information or situation could lead and spot possibilities that other people couldn't even begin to dream of. You are brilliant at coming up with flashes of inspiration for creative breakthroughs and crisis management.

## Mercury in Earth: Practical

Endless presentations of feelings, theories and possibilities can make your eyes glaze over and your brain ache to shut down. What really turns you on is trying out these theories and possibilities to see if they work in practice. If they don't, you'll tend to classify them 'of no further interest'. Emotionally charged information is at best a puzzling non-starter and at worst an irritating turn-off. Practical demonstrations, tried and tested facts and working models fascinate you. Hands-on learning, where you can see how a process functions from start to finish, especially if it leads to some useful material end-product, is right up your street. It's important to allow yourself plenty of time when you are learning, writing or thinking out what to say, otherwise you can feel rushed and out of control, never pleasant sensations for earth signs. Your special skill is in coming up with effective solutions to practical problems and in formulating long-range plans that bring concrete, measurable results.

## Mercury in Air: Logical
You love learning about, and playing with, ideas, theories and principles. Often you do this best by arguing or bouncing ideas off other people, or by writing down your thoughts. Your special gift is in your ability to stand back and work out the patterns of relationship between people or things. You much prefer it when facts are presented to you logically and unemotionally and have very little time for the irrational, uncertainty or for personal opinions. You do, though, tend to have plenty of those kinds of views yourself, only you call them logical conclusions. Whether a fact is useful or not is less important than whether it fits into your mental map of how the world operates. If facts don't fit in, you'll either ignore them, find a way of making them fit, or, occasionally, make a grand leap to a new, upgraded theory. Yours is the mind of the scientist or chess player. You make a brilliant planner because you can be detached enough to take an overview of the entire situation.

## Mercury in Water: Impressionable

Your mind is sensitive to atmospheres and emotional undertones and to the context in which information is presented. Plain facts and figures can often leave you cold and even intimidated. You can take things too personally and read between the lines for what you believe is really being said or taught. If you don't feel emotionally safe, you can be cautious about revealing your true thoughts. It may be hard, or even impossible, for you to learn properly in what you sense is a hostile environment. You are excellent at impression management. Like a skilful artist painting a picture, you can influence others to think what you'd like them to by using suggestive gestures or pauses and intonations. People with Mercury in water signs are often seriously disadvantaged by left-brain schooling methods that are too rigidly structured for them. You take in information best through pictures or images, so that you get a 'feel' for the material and can make an emotional bond with it, in the same way you connect with people. In emotionally supportive situations where there is a rapport between you and your instructors, or your learning material, you are able just to drink in and absorb circulating knowledge without conscious effort, sometimes not even being clear about how or why you know certain things.

## Finding Your Mercury Sign

If you don't yet know your Mercury sign, you might like to see if you can guess what it is from the descriptions below before checking it out in the tables on pp. 113–15.

## Sun in Libra with Mercury in Virgo

Jimmy Carter    Anna Ford    Graham Greene
Anne Robinson   Romy Schneider   Irvine Welsh

With critical and uncompromising Mercury in Virgo, you can use language like a precision instrument. You can fillet an opponent in the twinkling of an eye, as you are quick to spot the slightest flaw in them – or their arguments – and, if you choose, can pass comment to devastating effect. Writers with this placement have an eye for detail and are masters of meticulously crafted and clever plots. Sentences are polished and elegant, even if, as in the case of Irvine Welsh's *Trainspotting*, the subject matter is not.

Your normal approach to any task or situation is orderly, breaking the matter down into small, workable units. A habitual list-maker, you take pleasure in ticking off each item on paper, or in your imagination, as you have dealt with it. You enjoy ordering your information into neat mental filing cabinets and if you can't see how information can be put to some good use it won't hold your attention for long. With your eye and ear for practical detail and an interest in whether a thing will work or not in practice, you are more at home in the material world than most other Librans. Consequently, your plans and designs are usually down-to-earth and functional.

Sloppiness irritates you and you can be critical and sometimes rather sharp with yourself, and others, who don't live up to your exacting standards. You'll take a pride in communicating clearly and practically and can't bear waffling. In learning, teaching and communicating, your goal is excellence. That excellence is achieved by paying attention to every particular, discriminating and making choices at every turn, each one of which you are aware will affect the quality of your finished product.

## Sun in Libra with Mercury in Libra

| Melvyn Bragg | Bob Geldof | Vladimir Putin |
|---|---|---|
| Anita Roddick | Susan Sarandon | Margaret Thatcher |

You are excellent at strategic thinking and planning because you're capable of taking in the complexities of a situation, noticing especially if anyone isn't being given a fair hearing. This equips you well to make an excellent negotiator. You tend to be courteous and listen carefully to other people, agreeing with them frequently, to reassure them that you're on their side – even when you aren't and have quite different plans of your own up your sleeve. So you'll usually manage to get your way with the minimum of offence and the maximum of efficiency.

At times you may also be rather naive and idealistic, trying to see the best in everyone and every situation. With your charm and diplomacy, you rarely need to resort to direct confrontation, which is fortunate, as you prefer, wherever possible, to avoid unpleasantness. However, you dislike injustice even more and will use your considerable powers of persuasion to do what you can to right such wrongs. You are a natural debater, and rather enjoy the cut and thrust of verbal attack and counter-attack. To you, it is like playing a game of chess. Often you don't know what you think until you've aired a variety of positions and finally come to the one that seems to be the most balanced. You can find just the right words to be a peacemaker, but you may have to be careful not to say what people want to hear, just to please. Principles matter to you and, like

Margaret Thatcher, there is no way you will desert them, unless you are convinced that you were previously wrong. Then your sense of fairness will allow you to change over gracefully to the other side.

## Libra Sun with Mercury in Scorpio

Aleister Crowley  Edwina Currie   Heinrich Himmler
Cliff Richard      Marie Stopes    Oscar Wilde

Mercury in Scorpio can be expressed in a wide range of ways and, like everything else in Scorpio, the range can be extreme. You may simply prefer, like Cliff Richard, to keep your thoughts to yourself and be quietly but firmly protective of your privacy, whether or not you have anything to hide. There are others whose thoughts are obsessed with subjects that most people would prefer to avoid. Heinrich Himmler was the Nazi SS leader who planned and coordinated the systematic terrors, torture and slaughter of over seven million people, in and out of the concentration camps. Aleister Crowley loved to think of himself as the great beast 666 and was run out of Sicily because of alleged orgies and atrocities.

Money, control, sex and death are rarely far from your thoughts. *Married Love*, the book published by birth-control pioneer Marie Stopes in 1916 to counteract the misery caused by sexual ignorance, was banned in the USA. You could be a first-class sleuth or researcher, as, once you get interested in a subject, nothing about it is likely to escape your notice. You can spot cover-ups, scams and hypocrisy instantly – and you'll have no hesitation in speaking out either and exposing the matter if you feel it's necessary in the interests of justice – as Edwina Currie did when she revealed the levels of salmonella contamination in eggs, a fact that had previously been hushed up. You prefer to communicate in person, or by phone, because, that way, you can pick up subtle clues about what a person is feeling. Your mind tends to work in cycles: at times you'll be articulate, fluent and chatty, while at others you'll be withdrawn. That's the time for reading and thinking deeply, gathering resources for the future.

# NINE

# Venus — At Your Pleasure

♀ THE GLYPH FOR VENUS IS MADE UP OF THE CIRCLE OF ETERNITY on top of the cross of matter. Esoterically this represents love, which is a quality of the divine, revealed on earth through personal choice. The saying 'One man's meat is another man's poison' couldn't be more relevant when it comes to what we love. It is a mystery why we find one thing attractive and another unattractive, or even repulsive. Looking at the sign, aspects and house of your Venus can't give any explanation of this mystery, but it can give some clear indications of what it is that you value and find desirable. This can be quite different from what current fashion tells you you should like. For example, many people are strongly turned on by voluptuous bodies but the media constantly shows images of near-anorexics as the desirable ideal. If you ignore what you, personally, find beautiful and try to be, or to love, what at heart leaves you cold, you are setting yourself up for unnecessary pain and dissatisfaction. Being true to your Venus sign, even if other people think you are strange, brings joy and pleasure. It also builds up your self-esteem because it grounds you solidly in your own personal values. This, in turn, makes you much more attractive to others. Not only that, it improves your relationships immeasurably, because you are living authentically and not betraying yourself by trying to prove your worth to others by being something you are not.

Glittering Venus, the brightest planet in the heavens, was named after the goddess of love, war and victory. Earlier names for her were Aphrodite, Innana and Ishtar. She was beautiful, self-willed and self-indulgent but was also skilled in all the arts of civilisation.

Your Venus sign shows what you desire and would like to possess, not only in relationships but also in all aspects of your taste, from clothes and culture to hobbies and hobby-horses. It identifies how and where you can be charming and seductive and skilful at creating your own type of beauty yourself. It also describes your style of attracting partners and the kind of people that turn you on. When your Venus is activated you feel powerful, desirable and wonderfully, wickedly indulged and indulgent. When it is not, even if someone has all the right credentials to make a good match, the relationship will always lack that certain something. If you don't take the chance to express your Venus to a good enough degree somewhere in your life, you miss out woefully on delight and happiness.

## Morning Star, Evening Star

Venus appears in the sky either in the morning or in the evening. The ancients launched their attacks when Venus became a morning star, believing that she was then in her warrior-goddess role, releasing aggressive energy for victory in battle. If you're a morning-star person, you're likely to be impulsive, self-willed and idealistic, prepared to hold out until you find the partner who is just right for you.

Relationships and business dealings of morning-star Venus people are said to prosper best whenever Venus in the sky is a morning star. If you are an early bird, you can check this out. At these times Venus can be seen in the eastern sky before the Sun has risen.

The name for Venus as an evening star is Hesperus and it was then, traditionally, said to be sacred to lovers. Evening-star people tend to be easy-going and are open to negotiation, conciliation and making peace. If you are an evening-star Venus person, your best times in relationship and business affairs are said to be when Venus can be seen, jewel-like, in the western sky after the Sun has set.

Because the orbit of Venus is so close to the Sun, your Venus can only be in one of five signs. You have a morning-star Venus if your Venus is in one of the two signs that come before your Sun sign in the zodiac. You have an evening-star Venus if your Venus is in either of the two signs that follow your Sun sign. If you have Venus in the same sign as your Sun, you could be either, depending on whether your Venus is ahead of or behind your Sun. (You can find out which at the author's website www.janeridderpatrick.com.)

If you don't yet know your Venus sign, you might like to read through all of the following descriptions and see if you can guess what it is. You can find out for sure on pp. 116–18.

At the beginning of each section are the names of some well-known Librans with that particular Venus sign. You can find out more about them in Chapter Ten, Famous Libra Birthdays.

## Sun in Libra with Venus in Leo

Jimmy Carter    Truman Capote    Sebastian Coe
Carole Lombard  Olivia Newton-John  Gwyneth Paltrow

With a taste for luxury, only the finest will fit your bill. This could play havoc with your bank balance if you let it take over. You're in love with love and adore romantic gestures and high living – red roses and champagne and the finest clothes and jewellery. You'll enjoy rubbing shoulders with the rich and famous and almost invariably you're fun to be with and a thorough charmer. Truman Capote made a big impression by remembering people's names and tastes years after meeting them – and his *Breakfast at Tiffany's* is the epitome of elegant romance. You need a partner you can be proud of, as prestige matters to you, but you do like to be seen as special yourself. Honourable, noble and generous behaviour delights you and developing those qualities in yourself will bring you enormous satisfaction and improve the quality of all of your relationships, too.

This is an excellent placement for the worlds of art, theatre and fashion, as you have an impeccable flair for elegance, a gift for drama and an unshakeable belief in your own worth. To attract Clark Gable's attention, Carole Lombard once turned up at his party in an ambulance with sirens blaring, kitted out as an accident victim. Her attention-seeking stunts eventually won him over and they had what seems to have been an ideal marriage.

At best, you could be a first-class diplomat who values integrity and truth above all else. Since he left the White House, US president Jimmy Carter has worked tirelessly to improve international relations. Venus in Leo inclines to fidelity and Carter is probably one of the few American presidents not to have had a bit on the side, although, honest as ever, he did once confess to having committed adultery in his heart!

## Sun in Libra with Venus in Virgo

| Johnny Appleseed | Brigitte Bardot | Catherine Deneuve |
|---|---|---|
| Ray Kroc | Bob Geldof | Sarah Ferguson, Duchess of York |

According to Catherine Deneuve, to work is a noble art – and meaningful work is what you love above all. Take care, though, not to become a workaholic, putting your flesh-and-blood relationships at risk. You are at your happiest being of service, helping to improve the lives of others as Bob Geldof did with Band Aid and Brigitte Bardot does with her charity for distressed animals. Johnny Appleseed, a wandering man whose clothes were made of sackcloth and his hat a cooking pot, by the simple act of planting apple seeds wherever he went, over 49 years established flourishing orchards in five American states. With Virgo, it's the small but sustained efforts that add up to one magnificent whole.

Although Libra likes elegance, Venus in Virgo loves the useful. If your work involves the arts or design, you'll almost certainly be turned out meticulously. If dress isn't your focus, you could plump for the purely functional. You may not go as far as Johnny Appleseed, but at least two of the above celebrities would be unlikely candidates for a Best Dressed Person of the Year award. You take great pride in getting the details of whatever matters to you right. Ray Kroc founded McDonald's food chain, whose Virgoan formula for success is to 'define the basic premise of the service they offer, break the labour into constituent parts, and then continually reassemble and fine tune the many steps until the system works without a hitch'.

You need a partner whose mind and professionalism you can admire and respect and you may be quite critical of those who don't come up to your exacting standards. You are, however, willing to work on your relationships to become a devoted and supportive lover and partner.

## Sun in Libra with Venus in Libra

| Annie Besant | Melvyn Bragg | Terence Conran |
| Anita Roddick | Will Smith | Ann Widdecombe |

Libra men with Venus in Libra often have the elegance and empathy that is usually associated with women, but without in any way losing their masculinity – and may enjoy being a bit of a dandy. Women with this combination frequently combine hard-headed determination, cool thinking and firm principles with a pleasing exterior. You can be quite a tease, and with your smooth-talking tongue can flatter your way to success. Will Smith got the nickname of Prince from schoolmates, as he could always charm his way out of trouble. You like to feel liked and supported because genuine disharmony, or gross behaviour of any kind, can leave you sickened and deeply unhappy.

Your love of fairness may go far beyond the harmless vanities of personal appearance and take you into campaigning on behalf of those who are getting a raw deal by not being heard or represented. Annie Besant, concerned about the appalling conditions for women working in match factories, and about the lack of ethics in defrauding people of a fair wage in exchange for their labour, published the facts in *White Slavery in London*. She then helped the match girls form a union, and after a historic strike, Bryant & May were forced to make significant concessions.

In partnership, you like to feel you've met your equal and are usually willing to split the tasks 50–50 and not into the traditional male–female divisions of labour. For lasting happiness, it's important that you take a long, hard, realistic look at any potential partner, as you tend to see only what you choose to see around loved ones. Because of your tendency to try to mould your partner to match your ideal, it's best to choose one who is already close to it.

## Libra Sun with Venus in Scorpio

| Col. John Blashford-Snell | Edwina Currie | Diana Dors |
| Graham Greene | Irvine Welsh | Fred West |

Scorpio is the sign of extremes and you'd probably agree with the saying that if you're not living on the edge then you're taking up too much space. Despite your idealistic Libran nature that prefers to keep things 'nice', there is something that attracts you about the deeper, darker and more hidden side of life, as you hate hypocrisy and sham. Graham Greene wrestled in his novels with the nature of evil and Irvine Welsh exposed the sleazy underbelly of Edinburgh, one of the world's most elegant capitals. There's no way that you can stay pirouetting on the surface of life and you probably wouldn't want to anyway. Some love to push themselves into dangerous situations, like the explorer Col. Blashford-Snell, who led expeditions to uncover the secrets of hidden places, providing aid for conservation and medical services at the same time.

With your subtle and sultry sexuality, people can be magnetically drawn to you without being sure exactly why. You love to control, or to be controlled, and are attracted to partners who are powerful – either in personality or position – and who could be intense, wealthy, secretive or even slightly shady. Mysteries fascinate you and you are drawn to investigate and often to do something about it if corruption is involved. You may be possessive and jealous, though you're damned if you'll show it, and sometimes you may push your partner to the limits to see if they are trustworthy. You value your privacy and can be icy with those who, uninvited, would try to invade it. Sex is important, and if that doesn't work, the relationship could quickly sour. To be fulfilled, you need passion – either in love or in your love of work.

## Libra Sun with Venus in Sagittarius

| | | |
|---|---|---|
| Robert Atkins | Deepak Chopra | Evel Knievel |
| Aimee Semple McPherson | Paul Simon | Margaret Thatcher |

Sagittarius is the sign of showmanship, teaching, adventure and speculation and, in one form or another, those are the areas where you'll find your bliss. You probably love sports and risk-taking, though you may not be quite as much of a daredevil as Evel Knievel, the stuntman motorcyclist, unless, of course, you share the other more flamboyant and challenging parts of his chart.

Publicity and self-promotion can give you quite a buzz, and with your charming and strategic Libran Sun you'll know exactly how to present your mission and message in the best possible light. Whatever your gospel – and you're almost certain to have one – you'll take enormous pleasure in teaching and preaching it with zeal and conviction. Aimee Semple McPherson, the flamboyant American evangelist, used the media and drama to spread her pentecostal message. You have opinions and no way are you going to keep them to yourself. Margaret Thatcher evolved her own philosophy, which goes by the name of Thatcherism, based on free-market economics, increased personal responsibility and a smaller role for government – and the world soon knew about it. Robert Atkins made a fortune by publishing books about the controversial, but seemingly effective, low-carbohydrate diet he named after himself.

You may find yourself in the role of teacher or student with someone you love. Your partner may be connected with travel, sport, publishing or the legal profession. Being a free spirit, you hate to be tied down and, in any relationship, you need space to get on with exploring and promoting your own enthusiasms, as well as a partner who shares your beliefs. Foreign people, places and cultures could also fascinate you and travelling could be high on the list of priorities in your pursuit of pleasure.

# TEN

# Famous Libra Birthdays

FIND OUT WHO SHARES YOUR MOON, MERCURY AND VENUS SIGNS AND ANY challenging Sun aspects and see what they have done with the material they were born with. Notice how often it is not just the personalities of the people themselves but the roles of actors, characters of authors and works of artists that reflect their astrological make-up. In reading standard biographies, I've been constantly astounded – and, of course, delighted – at how often phrases used to describe individuals could have been lifted straight from their astrological profiles. Check it out yourself!

A few people below have been given a choice of two Moons. This is because the Moon changed sign on the day that they were born and no birth time was available. You may be able to guess which one is correct if you read the descriptions of the Moon signs in Chapter Seven.

## 23 September
1865 Baroness Emmuska Orczy, author, *The Scarlet Pimpernel*
Sun aspects: Uranus, Neptune
Moon: Scorpio   Mercury: Virgo   Venus: Leo

## 24 September
1896 F. Scott Fitzgerald, writer and playboy, *The Great Gatsby*
Sun aspects: none
Moon: Taurus   Mercury: Libra   Venus: Libra

## 25 September
1952 Christopher Reeve, actor, *Superman*, paralysed after a riding accident
Sun aspects: none
Moon: Sagittarius   Mercury: Libra   Venus: Libra

## 26 September
1888 T.S. Eliot, Nobel Prize-winning poet, *The Waste Land, Four Quartets*
Sun aspects: none
Moon: Gemini   Mercury: Libra   Venus: Libra

## 27 September
1957 Irvine Welsh, author, *Trainspotting* and *Porno*
Sun aspects: none
Moon: Scorpio   Mercury: Virgo   Venus: Scorpio

## 28 September
1934 Brigitte Bardot, French sex-kitten actress and animal rights campaigner
Sun aspects: none
Moon: Gemini   Mercury: Libra   Venus: Virgo

## 29 September
1758 Viscount Nelson, English admiral missing an eye and arm
Sun aspects: none
Moon: Virgo   Mercury: Libra   Venus: Virgo

## 30 September
1921 Deborah Kerr, actress in well-bred, ladylike roles, *From Here to Eternity*
Sun aspects: Saturn, Pluto
Moon: Virgo   Mercury: Scorpio   Venus: Virgo

## 1 October
1935 Julie Andrews, sunny actress, *Mary Poppins* and *The Sound of Music*
Sun aspects: none
Moon: Scorpio   Mercury: Scorpio   Venus: Virgo

## 2 October
1869 Mahatma Gandhi, Indian leader practising non-violent civil disobedience
Sun aspects: Neptune
Moon: Leo   Mercury: Scorpio   Venus: Scorpio

## 3 October
1925 Gore Vidal, American novelist, *Myra Breckenridge*, *Lincoln* and *Empire*
Sun aspects: Pluto
Moon: Aries   Mercury: Libra   Venus: Scorpio

## 4 October
1931 Terence Conran, English designer, founder of Habitat furnishing stores
Sun aspects: Saturn, Uranus
Moon: Gemini/Cancer   Mercury: Virgo   Venus: Libra

## 5 October
1902 Ray Kroc, founder of McDonald's fast food chain
Sun aspects: Saturn, Neptune
Moon: Scorpio/Sagittarius   Mercury: Scorpio   Venus: Virgo

## 6 October

1887 Le Corbusier, avante garde Swiss architect and designer
Sun aspects: Uranus
Moon: Gemini   Mercury: Scorpio   Venus: Virgo

## 7 October

1931 Archbishop Desmond Tutu, South African Nobel Peace Prize-winner
Sun aspects: Saturn, Uranus and Pluto
Moon: Leo   Mercury: Libra   Venus: Libra

## 8 October

1929 Betty Boothroyd, first woman Speaker of the House of Commons
Sun aspects: Uranus, Pluto
Moon: Sagittarius   Mercury: Libra   Venus: Virgo

## 9 October

1940 John Lennon, writer and artist, composer and singer with The Beatles
Sun aspects: none
Moon: Aquarius   Mercury: Scorpio   Venus: Virgo

## 10 October

1930 Harold Pinter, controversial English playwright, *The Birthday Party*
Sun aspects: Uranus, Pluto
Moon: Taurus   Mercury: Virgo   Venus: Scorpio

## 11 October

1884 Eleanor Roosevelt, gracious US First Lady, political activist and educator
Sun aspects: none
Moon: Cancer   Mercury: Libra   Venus: Virgo

## 12 October
1875 Aleister Crowley, self-proclaimed magician, *The Diary of a Drug Fiend*
Sun aspects: none
Moon: Pisces   Mercury: Scorpio   Venus: Libra

## 13 October
1925 Margaret Thatcher, first British woman prime minister
Sun aspects: Pluto
Moon: Leo   Mercury: Libra   Venus: Sagittarius

## 14 October
1940 Sir Cliff Richard, clean-cut popular singer, 'The Young Ones', 'Summer Holiday'
Sun aspects: none
Moon: Pisces/Aries   Mercury: Scorpio   Venus: Virgo

## 15 October
1800 Marie Stopes, birth control campaigner and educator
Sun aspects: Saturn
Moon: Pisces   Mercury: Scorpio   Venus: Scorpio

## 16 October
1854 Oscar Wilde, Irish playwright and wit, *The Importance of Being Earnest*
Sun aspects: none
Moon: Leo   Mercury: Scorpio   Venus: Libra

## 17 October
1938 Evel Knievel, exhibitionistic motorcycle stuntman who diced with death
Sun aspects: Saturn, Pluto
Moon: Leo   Mercury: Libra   Venus: Sagittarius

## 18 October
1939 Lee Harvey Oswald, alleged assassin of US president John F. Kennedy
Sun aspects: Saturn, Pluto
Moon: Capricorn   Mercury: Scorpio   Venus: Scorpio

## 19 October
1931 John le Carré, English thriller writer, *Tinker, Tailor, Soldier, Spy*
Sun aspects: Saturn, Uranus and Pluto
Moon: Aquarius   Mercury: Libra   Venus: Scorpio

## 20 October
1854 Arthur Rimbaud, French poet, *A Season in Hell*
Sun aspects: Pluto
Moon: Libra   Mercury: Scorpio   Venus: Libra

## 21 October
1940 Pelé, Brazilian footballer, considered to be world's best ever
Sun aspects: Pluto
Moon: Gemini   Mercury: Scorpio   Venus: Virgo

## 22 October
1943 Catherine Deneuve, elegant French actress with an ice-maiden manner
Sun aspects: none
Moon: Leo   Mercury: Libra   Venus: Virgo

## 23 October
1942 Anita Roddick, founder of The Body Shop ethical cosmetics empire
Sun aspects: Pluto
Moon: Aries   Mercury: Libra   Venus: Libra

## Other Libra people mentioned in this book

Queen Salawa Abeni, Nigerian Yoruba musical prodigy ☆ Johnny Appleseed, American folk hero ☆ Robert Atkins, promoter of a popular high-protein, low-carbohydrate diet ☆ Annie Besant, social activist, birth-control campaigner and theosophist ☆ Col. John Blashford-Snell, intrepid expedition leader ☆ Niels Bohr, Danish quantum theory physicist ☆ Marc Bolan, T. Rex singer, 'Ride a White Swan' ☆ Geoffrey Boycott, England cricketer ☆ Melvyn Bragg, author and broadcaster, *The South Bank Show* ☆ Chris de Burgh, singer, 'Lady in Red' ☆ Truman Capote, author, *Breakfast at Tiffany's* ☆ Jimmy Carter, US president ☆ Miguel de Cervantes, author, *Don Quixote* ☆ Chubby Checker, singer and inventor of 1960s dance craze 'The Twist' ☆ Deepak Chopra, alternative health doctor, *Ageless Body, Timeless Mind* ☆ Sebastian Coe, Olympic gold medal runner ☆ Michael Collins, Irish politician and Sinn Fein leader ☆ Edwina Currie, politician and writer, *A Parliamentary Affair* ☆ Jean-Claude van Damme, martial-arts actor, *Street Fighter* ☆ Matt Damon, actor and producer, *Good Will Hunting* ☆ Diana Dors, busty blonde actress, 'England's Marilyn Monroe' ☆ Lord Alfred Douglas, lover of Oscar Wilde ☆ Michael Douglas, actor and UN Messenger of Peace, *Traffic* ☆ Eminem, rap artist, *Slim Shady* ☆ Sarah Ferguson, Duchess of York, vivacious ex-wife of Prince Andrew ☆ Carrie Fisher, actress, *Star Wars* ☆ Anna Ford, elegant TV newsreader ☆ Bob Geldof, musician, with fellow Libran Midge Ure, Band Aid activist, 'Do They Know It's Christmas?' ☆ Graham Greene, author, *Our Man in Havana* ☆ Mark Hamill, actor, *Star Wars* ☆ Richard Harris, actor, Albus Dumbledore in *Harry Potter* ☆ Rita Hayworth, much-married actress and Second World War pin-up girl ☆ Jim Henson, creator of *The Muppets* ☆ Heinrich Himmler, Nazi police chief responsible for the butchery of over seven million people ☆ Jesse Jackson, American civil-rights leader ☆ Dr Samuel Johnson, man of letters and English dictionary compiler ☆

Catherine Zeta Jones, actress who shares a birthday with her husband Michael Douglas, *Traffic* ☆ Donna Karan, fashion designer ☆ Felicity Kendal, actress, *The Good Life* ☆ Alyn Kirk, actor, *Superman* ☆ R.D. Laing, controversial psychiatrist, *The Divided Self* ☆ Timothy Leary, 1960s psychedelic drugs guru who advocated 'turn on, tune in, drop out' ☆ Doris Lessing, author, *A Man and Two Women* ☆ Carole Lombard, actress, *Fast and Loose* ☆ Linda McCartney, vegetarian food producer and wife of Paul McCartney ☆ Ramsay MacDonald, outspoken first British Labour Prime Minister ☆ Aimee Semple McPherson, flamboyant American evangelist ☆ Katherine Mansfield, bohemian author who met, married and left her first husband within three weeks, *Prelude* ☆ Groucho Marx, wisecracking comedian, *Duck Soup* ☆ Arthur Miller, playwright once married to Marilyn Monroe, *Death of a Salesman* ☆ Roger Moore, smooth actor whose roles include James Bond and The Saint ☆ Olivia Newton-John, actress, *Grease* ☆ Friedrich Nietzsche, German philosopher, *Thus Spake Zarathustra* ☆ Alfred Nobel, Swedish chemist and founder of the Nobel prizes ☆ Gwyneth Paltrow, actress, *Shakespeare in Love* ☆ Luciano Pavarotti, Italian tenor ☆ Vladimir Putin, Russian president ☆ Anne Robinson, sharp-tongued quiz-show presenter, 'The Queen of Mean' ☆ Jennifer Rush, singer, 'The Power of Love' ☆ Susan Sarandon, actress, *Thelma and Louise* ☆ Paul Simon, musician, *Graceland* ☆ Will Smith, actor, *Men in Black* ☆ Bruce Springsteen, singer, *Born in the USA* ☆ Sting, singer and environmentalist, 'Every Breath You Take' ☆ Peter Stringfellow, nightclub-owner with large libido ☆ Midge Ure, musician and Band Aid activist, 'Do They Know It's Christmas?' ☆ Fred West, brutal sex murderer ☆ Ann Widdecombe, tough-minded Tory politician ☆ Serena Williams, triple grand slam-winnning tennis player ☆ Kate Winslet, actress, *Titanic* ☆ P.G. Wodehouse, author and creator of Bertie Wooster

# ELEVEN

# Finding Your Sun, Moon, Mercury and Venus Signs

ALL OF THE ASTROLOGICAL DATA IN THIS BOOK WAS CALCULATED by Astrolabe, who also supply a wide range of astrological software. I am most grateful for their help and generosity.

ASTROLABE, PO Box 1750, Brewster, MA 02631, USA
www.alabe.com

PLEASE NOTE THAT ALL OF THE TIMES GIVEN ARE IN GREENWICH MEAN TIME (GMT). If you were born during British Summer Time (BST) you will need to subtract one hour from your birth time to convert it to GMT. If you were born outside of the British Isles, find the time zone of your place of birth and the number of hours it is different from GMT. Add the difference in hours if you were born west of the UK, and subtract the difference if you were born east of the UK to convert your birth time to GMT.

## Your Sun Sign

Check your year of birth, and if you were born between the dates and times given the Sun was in Libra when you were born – confirming that you're a Libran. If you were born before the time on the date that Libra begins in your year, you are a Virgo. If you were born after the time on the date Libra ends in your year, you are a Scorpio.

## Your Moon Sign

The Moon changes sign every two and a half days. To find your Moon sign, first find your year of birth. You will notice that in each year box there are three columns.

The second column shows the day of the month that the Moon changed sign, while the first column gives the abbreviation for the sign that the Moon entered on that date.

In the middle column, the month has been omitted, so that the dates run from, for example, 23 to 30 (September) and then from 1 to 23 (October).

In the third column, after the star, the time that the Moon changed sign on that day is given.

Look down the middle column of your year box to find your date of birth. If your birth date is given, look to the third column to find the time that the Moon changed sign. If you were born after that time, your Moon sign is given in the first column next to your birth date. If you were born before that time, your Moon sign is the one above the one next to your birth date.

If your birth date is not given, find the closest date before it. The sign shown next to that date is your Moon sign.

If you were born on a day that the Moon changed signs and you do not know your time of birth, try out both of that day's Moon signs and feel which one fits you best.

The abbreviations for the signs are as follows:

Aries – Ari     Taurus – Tau     Gemini – Gem     Cancer – Can
Leo – Leo     Virgo – Vir     Libra – Lib     Scorpio – Sco
Sagittarius – Sag  Capricorn – Cap  Aquarius – Aqu  Pisces – Pis

## Your Mercury Sign

Find your year of birth and then the column in which your birthday falls. Look up to the top of the column to find your Mercury sign. You will see that some dates appear twice. This is because Mercury changed sign that day. If your birthday falls on one of these dates, try out both Mercury signs and see which one fits you best. If you know your birth time, you can find out for sure which Mercury sign is yours on my website – www.janeridderpatrick.com.

## Your Venus Sign

Find your year of birth and then the column in which your birthday falls. Look up to the top of the column to find your Venus sign. Some dates have two possible signs. That's because Venus changed signs that day. Try them both out and see which fits you best. If the year you are interested in doesn't appear in the tables, or you have Venus in the same sign as your Sun and want to know whether you have a morning or evening star Venus, you can find the information on my website – www.janeridderpatrick.com.

## ♎ Libra Sun Tables ☉

| YEAR | LIBRA BEGINS | LIBRA ENDS |
|---|---|---|
| 1930 | 23 Sep 18.35 | 24 Oct 03.25 |
| 1931 | 24 Sep 00.23 | 24 Oct 09.15 |
| 1932 | 23 Sep 06.15 | 23 Oct 15.03 |
| 1933 | 23 Sep 12.01 | 23 Oct 20.48 |
| 1934 | 23 Sep 17.45 | 24 Oct 02.36 |
| 1935 | 23 Sep 23.38 | 24 Oct 08.29 |
| 1936 | 23 Sep 05.25 | 23 Oct 14.18 |
| 1937 | 23 Sep 11.12 | 23 Oct 20.06 |
| 1938 | 23 Sep 16.59 | 24 Oct 01.53 |
| 1939 | 23 Sep 22.49 | 24 Oct 07.45 |
| 1940 | 23 Sep 04.45 | 23 Oct 13.39 |
| 1941 | 23 Sep 10.32 | 23 Oct 19.27 |
| 1942 | 23 Sep 16.16 | 24 Oct 01.15 |
| 1943 | 23 Sep 22.11 | 24 Oct 07.08 |
| 1944 | 23 Sep 04.01 | 23 Oct 12.55 |
| 1945 | 23 Sep 09.49 | 23 Oct 18.43 |
| 1946 | 23 Sep 15.40 | 24 Oct 00.34 |
| 1947 | 23 Sep 21.28 | 24 Oct 06.25 |
| 1948 | 23 Sep 03.21 | 23 Oct 12.18 |
| 1949 | 23 Sep 09.05 | 23 Oct 18.02 |
| 1950 | 23 Sep 14.43 | 23 Oct 23.44 |
| 1951 | 23 Sep 20.36 | 24 Oct 05.35 |
| 1952 | 23 Sep 02.23 | 23 Oct 11.22 |
| 1953 | 23 Sep 13.55 | 23 Oct 17.06 |
| 1954 | 23 Sep 13.55 | 23 Oct 22.56 |
| 1955 | 23 Sep 19.40 | 24 Oct 04.42 |
| 1956 | 23 Sep 01.34 | 23 Oct 10.34 |
| 1957 | 23 Sep 07.26 | 23 Oct 16.24 |
| 1958 | 23 Sep 13.08 | 23 Oct 22.11 |
| 1959 | 23 Sep 19.08 | 24 Oct 04.10 |
| 1960 | 23 Sep 00.58 | 23 Oct 10.01 |
| 1961 | 23 Sep 06.42 | 23 Oct 15.47 |
| 1962 | 23 Sep 12.35 | 23 Oct 21.39 |
| 1963 | 23 Sep 18.23 | 24 Oct 03.28 |

| YEAR | LIBRA BEGINS | LIBRA ENDS |
|------|--------------|------------|
| 1964 | 23 Sep 00.16 | 23 Oct 09.20 |
| 1965 | 23 Sep 06.05 | 23 Oct 15.09 |
| 1966 | 23 Sep 11.43 | 23 Oct 20.50 |
| 1967 | 23 Sep 17.37 | 24 Oct 02.43 |
| 1968 | 22 Sep 23.26 | 23 Oct 08.29 |
| 1969 | 23 Sep 05.06 | 23 Oct 14.11 |
| 1970 | 23 Sep 10.58 | 23 Oct 20.04 |
| 1971 | 23 Sep 16.44 | 24 Oct 01.53 |
| 1972 | 22 Sep 22.32 | 23 Oct 07.41 |
| 1973 | 23 Sep 04.21 | 23 Oct 13.30 |
| 1974 | 23 Sep 09.58 | 23 Oct 19.10 |
| 1975 | 23 Sep 15.55 | 24 Oct 01.05 |
| 1976 | 22 Sep 21.48 | 23 Oct 06.57 |
| 1977 | 23 Sep 03.29 | 23 Oct 12.40 |
| 1978 | 23 Sep 09.25 | 23 Oct 18.37 |
| 1979 | 23 Sep 15.16 | 24 Oct 00.27 |
| 1980 | 22 Sep 21.08 | 23 Oct 06.17 |
| 1981 | 23 Sep 03.05 | 23 Oct 12.12 |
| 1982 | 23 Sep 08.46 | 23 Oct 17.57 |
| 1983 | 23 Sep 14.41 | 23 Oct 23.54 |
| 1984 | 22 Sep 20.32 | 23 Oct 05.45 |
| 1985 | 23 Sep 02.07 | 23 Oct 11.21 |
| 1986 | 23 Sep 07.58 | 23 Oct 17.14 |
| 1987 | 23 Sep 13.45 | 23 Oct 23.00 |
| 1988 | 22 Sep 19.28 | 23 Oct 04.44 |
| 1989 | 23 Sep 01.19 | 23 Oct 10.35 |
| 1990 | 23 Sep 06.55 | 23 Oct 16.13 |
| 1991 | 23 Sep 12.48 | 23 Oct 22.05 |
| 1992 | 22 Sep 18.42 | 23 Oct 03.47 |
| 1993 | 23 Sep 00.22 | 23 Oct 09.37 |
| 1994 | 23 Sep 06.19 | 23 Oct 15.35 |
| 1995 | 23 Sep 12.12 | 23 Oct 21.31 |
| 1996 | 22 Sep 18.00 | 23 Oct 03.18 |
| 1997 | 22 Sep 05.37 | 23 Oct 14.58 |
| 1998 | 23 Sep 23.55 | 23 Oct 14.58 |
| 1999 | 23 Sep 11.31 | 23 Oct 20.52 |
| 2000 | 22 Sep 17.27 | 23 Oct 02.47 |

♎ Libra – Finding Your Moon Sign ☽

| 1930 | | |
|---|---|---|
| Sco | 24 | *15:08 |
| Sag | 26 | *19:34 |
| Cap | 29 | *03:48 |
| Aqu | 1 | *15:09 |
| Pis | 4 | *03:47 |
| Ari | 6 | *15:51 |
| Tau | 9 | *02:13 |
| Gem | 11 | *10:28 |
| Can | 13 | *16:28 |
| Leo | 15 | *20:18 |
| Vir | 17 | *22:25 |
| Lib | 19 | *23:43 |
| Sco | 22 | *01:33 |

| 1931 | | |
|---|---|---|
| Pis | 24 | *01:28 |
| Ari | 26 | *14:09 |
| Tau | 29 | *03:06 |
| Gem | 1 | *15:02 |
| Can | 4 | *00:36 |
| Leo | 6 | *06:48 |
| Vir | 8 | *09:33 |
| Lib | 10 | *09:49 |
| Sco | 12 | *09:17 |
| Sag | 14 | *09:52 |
| Cap | 16 | *13:19 |
| Aqu | 18 | *20:39 |
| Pis | 21 | *07:32 |

| 1932 | | |
|---|---|---|
| Can | 23 | *01:12 |
| Leo | 25 | *10:30 |
| Vir | 27 | *16:05 |
| Lib | 29 | *18:21 |
| Sco | 1 | *18:43 |
| Sag | 3 | *19:02 |
| Cap | 5 | *21:00 |
| Aqu | 8 | *01:44 |
| Pis | 10 | *09:26 |
| Ari | 12 | *19:35 |
| Tau | 15 | *07:23 |
| Gem | 17 | *20:02 |
| Can | 20 | *08:25 |
| Leo | 22 | *18:56 |

| 1933 | | |
|---|---|---|
| Sag | 24 | *07:48 |
| Cap | 26 | *10:23 |
| Aqu | 28 | *13:26 |
| Pis | 30 | *17:26 |
| Ari | 2 | *22:51 |
| Tau | 5 | *06:17 |
| Gem | 7 | *16:18 |
| Can | 10 | *04:29 |
| Leo | 12 | *17:01 |
| Vir | 15 | *03:23 |
| Lib | 17 | *10:06 |
| Sco | 19 | *13:26 |
| Sag | 21 | *14:53 |

| 1934 | | |
|---|---|---|
| Ari | 23 | *05:13 |
| Tau | 25 | *07:47 |
| Gem | 27 | *13:34 |
| Can | 29 | *23:15 |
| Leo | 2 | *11:44 |
| Vir | 5 | *00:30 |
| Lib | 7 | *11:19 |
| Sco | 9 | *19:31 |
| Sag | 12 | *01:31 |
| Cap | 14 | *06:03 |
| Aqu | 16 | *09:31 |
| Pis | 18 | *12:09 |
| Ari | 20 | *14:28 |
| Tau | 22 | *17:34 |

♎ Libra – Finding Your Moon Sign ☽

| 1935 | | | 1936 | | | 1937 | | | 1938 | | | 1939 | | |
|---|---|---|---|---|---|---|---|---|---|---|---|---|---|---|
| Vir | 24 | *21:18 | Cap | 23 | *20:52 | Gem | 24 | *20:46 | Lib | 23 | *20:19 | Aqu | 23 | *04:24 |
| Lib | 27 | *10:05 | Aqu | 26 | *04:52 | Can | 26 | *23:24 | Sco | 26 | *00:57 | Pis | 25 | *16:59 |
| Sco | 29 | *22:05 | Pis | 28 | *08:38 | Leo | 29 | *03:14 | Sag | 28 | *09:02 | Ari | 28 | *05:21 |
| Sag | 2 | *08:40 | Ari | 30 | *09:09 | Vir | 1 | *08:29 | Cap | 30 | *20:20 | Tau | 30 | *16:28 |
| Cap | 4 | *17:02 | Tau | 2 | *08:25 | Lib | 3 | *15:31 | Aqu | 3 | *08:57 | Gem | 3 | *01:37 |
| Aqu | 6 | *22:19 | Gem | 4 | *08:37 | Sco | 6 | *00:55 | Pis | 5 | *20:26 | Can | 5 | *08:15 |
| Pis | 9 | *00:25 | Can | 6 | *11:29 | Sag | 8 | *12:44 | Ari | 8 | *05:22 | Leo | 7 | *12:08 |
| Ari | 11 | *00:19 | Leo | 8 | *17:44 | Cap | 11 | *01:46 | Tau | 10 | *11:41 | Vir | 9 | *13:45 |
| Tau | 12 | *23:54 | Vir | 11 | *03:01 | Aqu | 13 | *13:36 | Gem | 12 | *16:09 | Lib | 11 | *14:15 |
| Gem | 15 | *01:18 | Lib | 13 | *14:19 | Pis | 15 | *22:01 | Can | 14 | *19:30 | Sco | 13 | *15:18 |
| Can | 17 | *06:20 | Sco | 16 | *02:46 | Ari | 18 | *02:31 | Leo | 16 | *22:19 | Sag | 15 | *18:36 |
| Leo | 19 | *15:35 | Sag | 18 | *15:37 | Tau | 20 | *04:09 | Vir | 19 | *01:09 | Cap | 18 | *01:22 |
| Vir | 22 | *03:44 | Cap | 21 | *03:36 | Gem | 22 | *04:39 | Lib | 21 | *04:43 | Aqu | 20 | *11:40 |

100

♎ Libra – Finding Your Moon Sign ☽

**1940**
| | | |
|---|---|---|
| Can | 24 | *14:56 |
| Leo | 26 | *21:07 |
| Vir | 28 | *23:40 |
| Lib | 30 | *23:46 |
| Sco | 2 | *23:12 |
| Sag | 4 | *23:55 |
| Cap | 7 | *03:29 |
| Aqu | 9 | *10:44 |
| Pis | 11 | *21:18 |
| Ari | 14 | *09:50 |
| Tau | 16 | *22:48 |
| Gem | 19 | *10:58 |
| Can | 21 | *21:17 |

**1941**
| | | |
|---|---|---|
| Sco | 23 | *09:23 |
| Sag | 25 | *10:24 |
| Cap | 27 | *12:45 |
| Aqu | 29 | *17:16 |
| Pis | 2 | *00:18 |
| Ari | 4 | *09:37 |
| Tau | 6 | *20:51 |
| Gem | 9 | *09:22 |
| Can | 11 | *21:52 |
| Leo | 14 | *08:28 |
| Vir | 16 | *15:35 |
| Lib | 18 | *18:53 |
| Sco | 20 | *19:25 |
| Sag | 22 | *19:00 |

**1942**
| | | |
|---|---|---|
| Ari | 24 | *12:57 |
| Tau | 26 | *19:34 |
| Gem | 29 | *05:05 |
| Can | 1 | *17:03 |
| Leo | 4 | *05:35 |
| Vir | 6 | *16:12 |
| Lib | 8 | *23:31 |
| Sco | 11 | *03:45 |
| Sag | 13 | *06:10 |
| Cap | 15 | *08:13 |
| Aqu | 17 | *11:01 |
| Pis | 19 | *15:05 |
| Ari | 21 | *20:36 |

**1943**
| | | |
|---|---|---|
| Leo | 24 | *00:33 |
| Vir | 26 | *13:29 |
| Lib | 29 | *00:55 |
| Sco | 1 | *10:03 |
| Sag | 3 | *17:02 |
| Cap | 5 | *22:10 |
| Aqu | 8 | *01:38 |
| Pis | 10 | *03:44 |
| Ari | 12 | *05:11 |
| Tau | 14 | *07:26 |
| Gem | 16 | *12:08 |
| Can | 18 | *20:28 |
| Leo | 21 | *08:12 |

**1944**
| | | |
|---|---|---|
| Cap | 25 | *07:54 |
| Aqu | 27 | *13:08 |
| Pis | 29 | *14:56 |
| Ari | 1 | *14:29 |
| Tau | 3 | *13:46 |
| Gem | 5 | *15:00 |
| Can | 7 | *19:56 |
| Leo | 10 | *05:03 |
| Vir | 12 | *17:04 |
| Lib | 15 | *05:55 |
| Sco | 17 | *18:03 |
| Sag | 20 | *04:49 |
| Cap | 22 | *13:47 |

| 1945 | | |
|---|---|---|
| Tau | 23 | *22:53 |
| Gem | 25 | *23:32 |
| Can | 28 | *02:39 |
| Leo | 30 | *08:47 |
| Vir | 2 | *17:33 |
| Lib | 5 | *04:16 |
| Sco | 7 | *16:23 |
| Sag | 10 | *05:17 |
| Cap | 12 | *17:32 |
| Aqu | 15 | *03:05 |
| Pis | 17 | *08:32 |
| Ari | 19 | *10:08 |
| Tau | 21 | *09:30 |

| 1946 | | |
|---|---|---|
| Lib | 25 | *05:40 |
| Sco | 27 | *14:12 |
| Sag | 30 | *01:32 |
| Cap | 2 | *14:28 |
| Aqu | 5 | *02:26 |
| Pis | 7 | *11:07 |
| Ari | 9 | *16:04 |
| Tau | 11 | *18:20 |
| Gem | 13 | *19:36 |
| Can | 15 | *21:23 |
| Leo | 18 | *00:35 |
| Vir | 20 | *05:35 |
| Lib | 22 | *12:33 |

| 1947 | | |
|---|---|---|
| Aqu | 24 | *21:37 |
| Pis | 27 | *09:23 |
| Ari | 29 | *18:57 |
| Tau | 2 | *02:14 |
| Gem | 4 | *07:43 |
| Can | 6 | *11:46 |
| Leo | 8 | *14:41 |
| Vir | 10 | *16:56 |
| Lib | 12 | *19:31 |
| Sco | 14 | *23:46 |
| Sag | 17 | *06:52 |
| Cap | 19 | *17:14 |
| Aqu | 22 | *05:38 |

| 1948 | | |
|---|---|---|
| Gem | 23 | *16:39 |
| Can | 25 | *23:44 |
| Leo | 28 | *03:34 |
| Vir | 30 | *04:40 |
| Lib | 2 | *04:30 |
| Sco | 4 | *04:58 |
| Sag | 6 | *07:55 |
| Cap | 8 | *14:31 |
| Aqu | 11 | *00:42 |
| Pis | 13 | *13:03 |
| Ari | 16 | *01:35 |
| Tau | 18 | *12:53 |
| Gem | 20 | *22:13 |

| 1949 | | |
|---|---|---|
| Sco | 24 | *13:21 |
| Sag | 26 | *14:21 |
| Cap | 28 | *18:06 |
| Aqu | 1 | *01:14 |
| Pis | 3 | *11:20 |
| Ari | 5 | *23:27 |
| Tau | 8 | *12:26 |
| Gem | 11 | *01:01 |
| Can | 13 | *11:49 |
| Leo | 15 | *19:34 |
| Vir | 17 | *23:41 |
| Lib | 20 | *00:46 |
| Sco | 22 | *00:18 |

| 1950 | | |
|---|---|---|
| Pis | 23 | *15:09 |
| Ari | 25 | *23:32 |
| Tau | 28 | *10:08 |
| Gem | 30 | *22:26 |
| Can | 3 | *10:58 |
| Leo | 5 | *21:38 |
| Vir | 8 | *04:53 |
| Lib | 10 | *08:28 |
| Sco | 12 | *09:30 |
| Sag | 14 | *09:44 |
| Cap | 16 | *10:55 |
| Aqu | 18 | *14:27 |
| Pis | 20 | *20:53 |

| 1951 | | |
|---|---|---|
| Can | 23 | *05:34 |
| Leo | 25 | *18:07 |
| Vir | 28 | *05:05 |
| Lib | 30 | *13:07 |
| Sco | 2 | *18:23 |
| Sag | 4 | *21:47 |
| Cap | 7 | *00:29 |
| Aqu | 9 | *03:19 |
| Pis | 11 | *06:46 |
| Ari | 13 | *11:20 |
| Tau | 15 | *17:37 |
| Gem | 18 | *02:22 |
| Can | 20 | *13:42 |

| 1952 | | |
|---|---|---|
| Sag | 24 | *08:32 |
| Cap | 26 | *14:05 |
| Aqu | 28 | *17:24 |
| Pis | 30 | *18:52 |
| Ari | 2 | *19:33 |
| Tau | 4 | *21:06 |
| Gem | 7 | *01:16 |
| Can | 9 | *09:16 |
| Leo | 11 | *20:50 |
| Vir | 14 | *09:50 |
| Lib | 16 | *21:43 |
| Sco | 19 | *07:09 |
| Sag | 21 | *14:11 |

| 1953 | | |
|---|---|---|
| Ari | 23 | *04:30 |
| Tau | 25 | *03:45 |
| Gem | 27 | *05:01 |
| Can | 29 | *09:57 |
| Leo | 1 | *18:53 |
| Vir | 4 | *06:40 |
| Lib | 6 | *19:27 |
| Sco | 9 | *07:55 |
| Sag | 11 | *19:18 |
| Cap | 14 | *04:51 |
| Aqu | 16 | *11:32 |
| Pis | 18 | *14:54 |
| Ari | 20 | *15:26 |
| Tau | 22 | *14:46 |

| 1954 | | |
|---|---|---|
| Vir | 24 | *08:10 |
| Lib | 26 | *18:10 |
| Sco | 29 | *05:51 |
| Sag | 1 | *18:41 |
| Cap | 4 | *07:03 |
| Aqu | 6 | *16:44 |
| Pis | 8 | *22:15 |
| Ari | 10 | *23:57 |
| Tau | 12 | *23:31 |
| Gem | 14 | *23:10 |
| Can | 17 | *00:51 |
| Leo | 19 | *05:41 |
| Vir | 21 | *13:45 |

♎ Libra – Finding Your Moon Sign ☽

| 1955 | | |
|---|---|---|
| Cap | 24 | *03:00 |
| Aqu | 26 | *15:06 |
| Pis | 29 | *00:11 |
| Ari | 1 | *05:46 |
| Tau | 3 | *08:51 |
| Gem | 5 | *10:59 |
| Can | 7 | *13:22 |
| Leo | 9 | *16:41 |
| Vir | 11 | *21:11 |
| Lib | 14 | *03:13 |
| Sco | 16 | *11:24 |
| Sag | 18 | *22:08 |
| Cap | 21 | *10:51 |

| 1956 | | |
|---|---|---|
| Gem | 24 | *23:24 |
| Can | 27 | *03:59 |
| Leo | 29 | *06:48 |
| Vir | 1 | *08:24 |
| Lib | 3 | *10:01 |
| Sco | 5 | *13:20 |
| Sag | 7 | *19:46 |
| Cap | 10 | *05:47 |
| Aqu | 12 | *18:09 |
| Pis | 15 | *06:24 |
| Ari | 17 | *16:34 |
| Tau | 20 | *00:06 |
| Gem | 22 | *05:28 |

| 1957 | | |
|---|---|---|
| Lib | 23 | *18:32 |
| Sco | 25 | *18:40 |
| Sag | 27 | *21:28 |
| Cap | 30 | *03:59 |
| Aqu | 2 | *14:04 |
| Pis | 5 | *02:17 |
| Ari | 7 | *14:56 |
| Tau | 10 | *02:47 |
| Gem | 12 | *12:59 |
| Can | 14 | *20:53 |
| Leo | 17 | *01:58 |
| Vir | 19 | *04:23 |
| Lib | 21 | *05:02 |

| 1958 | | |
|---|---|---|
| Pis | 25 | *01:33 |
| Ari | 27 | *13:07 |
| Tau | 30 | *01:57 |
| Gem | 2 | *14:49 |
| Can | 5 | *01:59 |
| Leo | 7 | *09:49 |
| Vir | 9 | *13:48 |
| Lib | 11 | *14:43 |
| Sco | 13 | *14:11 |
| Sag | 15 | *14:09 |
| Cap | 17 | *16:23 |
| Aqu | 19 | *22:05 |
| Pis | 22 | *07:19 |

| 1959 | | |
|---|---|---|
| Can | 24 | *23:48 |
| Leo | 27 | *10:35 |
| Vir | 29 | *18:03 |
| Lib | 1 | *22:07 |
| Sco | 3 | *23:53 |
| Sag | 6 | *00:54 |
| Cap | 8 | *02:38 |
| Aqu | 10 | *06:12 |
| Pis | 12 | *12:06 |
| Ari | 14 | *20:20 |
| Tau | 17 | *06:39 |
| Gem | 19 | *18:39 |
| Can | 22 | *07:22 |

**1960**

| | | |
|---|---|---|
| Sco | 23 | *09:17 |
| Sag | 25 | *13:41 |
| Cap | 27 | *16:53 |
| Aqu | 29 | *19:32 |
| Pis | 1 | *22:14 |
| Ari | 4 | *01:46 |
| Tau | 6 | *07:09 |
| Gem | 8 | *15:17 |
| Can | 11 | *02:18 |
| Leo | 13 | *14:54 |
| Vir | 16 | *02:39 |
| Lib | 18 | *11:31 |
| Sco | 20 | *17:05 |
| Sag | 22 | *20:15 |

**1961**

| | | |
|---|---|---|
| Ari | 24 | *09:40 |
| Tau | 26 | *10:42 |
| Gem | 28 | *14:32 |
| Can | 30 | *22:20 |
| Leo | 3 | *09:43 |
| Vir | 5 | *22:45 |
| Lib | 8 | *11:03 |
| Sco | 10 | *21:18 |
| Sag | 13 | *05:20 |
| Cap | 15 | *11:22 |
| Aqu | 17 | *15:36 |
| Pis | 19 | *18:09 |
| Ari | 21 | *19:35 |

**1962**

| | | |
|---|---|---|
| Leo | 23 | *09:07 |
| Vir | 25 | *20:30 |
| Lib | 28 | *09:07 |
| Sco | 30 | *21:48 |
| Sag | 3 | *09:39 |
| Cap | 5 | *19:34 |
| Aqu | 8 | *02:20 |
| Pis | 10 | *05:28 |
| Ari | 12 | *05:40 |
| Tau | 14 | *04:43 |
| Gem | 16 | *04:50 |
| Can | 18 | *08:05 |
| Leo | 20 | *15:30 |

**1963**

| | | |
|---|---|---|
| Sag | 23 | *07:49 |
| Cap | 25 | *20:14 |
| Aqu | 28 | *06:03 |
| Pis | 30 | *11:44 |
| Ari | 2 | *13:47 |
| Tau | 4 | *13:49 |
| Gem | 6 | *13:58 |
| Can | 8 | *16:01 |
| Leo | 10 | *20:54 |
| Vir | 13 | *04:34 |
| Lib | 15 | *14:24 |
| Sco | 18 | *01:52 |
| Sag | 20 | *14:32 |

**1964**

| | | |
|---|---|---|
| Tau | 23 | *23:45 |
| Gem | 26 | *02:45 |
| Can | 28 | *05:39 |
| Leo | 30 | *08:52 |
| Vir | 2 | *12:42 |
| Lib | 4 | *17:44 |
| Sco | 7 | *00:57 |
| Sag | 9 | *11:02 |
| Cap | 11 | *23:31 |
| Aqu | 14 | *12:14 |
| Pis | 16 | *22:31 |
| Ari | 19 | *05:04 |
| Tau | 21 | *08:23 |

♎ Libra – Finding Your Moon Sign ☽

| 1965 | | |
|---|---|---|
| Lib | 25 | *00:16 |
| Sco | 27 | *02:47 |
| Sag | 29 | *08:42 |
| Cap | 1 | *18:28 |
| Aqu | 4 | *06:48 |
| Pis | 6 | *19:13 |
| Ari | 9 | *05:53 |
| Tau | 11 | *14:15 |
| Gem | 13 | *20:39 |
| Can | 16 | *01:26 |
| Leo | 18 | *04:50 |
| Vir | 20 | *07:13 |
| Lib | 22 | *09:21 |

| 1966 | | |
|---|---|---|
| Aqu | 24 | *03:48 |
| Pis | 26 | *15:48 |
| Ari | 29 | *04:29 |
| Tau | 1 | *16:46 |
| Gem | 4 | *03:42 |
| Can | 6 | *12:11 |
| Leo | 8 | *17:24 |
| Vir | 10 | *19:26 |
| Lib | 12 | *19:29 |
| Sco | 14 | *19:21 |
| Sag | 16 | *21:00 |
| Cap | 19 | *01:56 |
| Aqu | 21 | *10:41 |

| 1967 | | |
|---|---|---|
| Gem | 24 | *04:20 |
| Can | 26 | *15:44 |
| Leo | 28 | *23:39 |
| Vir | 1 | *03:37 |
| Lib | 3 | *04:33 |
| Sco | 5 | *04:14 |
| Sag | 7 | *04:32 |
| Cap | 9 | *07:03 |
| Aqu | 11 | *12:46 |
| Pis | 13 | *21:38 |
| Ari | 16 | *08:57 |
| Tau | 18 | *21:41 |
| Gem | 21 | *10:37 |

| 1968 | | |
|---|---|---|
| Sco | 24 | *14:38 |
| Sag | 26 | *16:30 |
| Cap | 28 | *18:44 |
| Aqu | 30 | *22:11 |
| Pis | 3 | *03:21 |
| Ari | 5 | *10:35 |
| Tau | 7 | *20:06 |
| Gem | 10 | *07:43 |
| Can | 12 | *20:23 |
| Leo | 15 | *08:07 |
| Vir | 17 | *16:58 |
| Lib | 19 | *22:03 |
| Sco | 22 | *00:04 |

| 1969 | | |
|---|---|---|
| Pis | 23 | *13:22 |
| Ari | 25 | *15:55 |
| Tau | 27 | *20:29 |
| Gem | 30 | *04:05 |
| Can | 2 | *14:52 |
| Leo | 5 | *03:24 |
| Vir | 7 | *15:20 |
| Lib | 10 | *00:47 |
| Sco | 12 | *07:18 |
| Sag | 14 | *11:32 |
| Cap | 16 | *14:35 |
| Aqu | 18 | *17:20 |
| Pis | 20 | *20:25 |

♎ Libra – Finding Your Moon Sign ☽

| 1970 | | |
|---|---|---|
| Leo | 24 | *22:54 |
| Vir | 27 | *11:53 |
| Lib | 30 | *00:32 |
| Sco | 2 | *11:34 |
| Sag | 4 | *20:30 |
| Cap | 7 | *03:09 |
| Aqu | 9 | *07:25 |
| Pis | 11 | *09:29 |
| Ari | 13 | *10:11 |
| Tau | 15 | *11:00 |
| Gem | 17 | *13:44 |
| Can | 19 | *19:59 |
| Leo | 22 | *06:12 |

| 1971 | | |
|---|---|---|
| Sag | 24 | *23:42 |
| Cap | 27 | *09:51 |
| Aqu | 29 | *16:38 |
| Pis | 1 | *19:35 |
| Ari | 3 | *19:40 |
| Tau | 5 | *18:41 |
| Gem | 7 | *18:53 |
| Can | 9 | *22:11 |
| Leo | 12 | *05:30 |
| Vir | 14 | *16:16 |
| Lib | 17 | *04:47 |
| Sco | 19 | *17:30 |
| Sag | 22 | *05:31 |

| 1972 | | |
|---|---|---|
| Ari | 23 | *03:43 |
| Tau | 25 | *04:27 |
| Gem | 27 | *05:14 |
| Can | 29 | *07:38 |
| Leo | 1 | *12:26 |
| Vir | 3 | *19:30 |
| Lib | 6 | *04:34 |
| Sco | 8 | *15:27 |
| Sag | 11 | *03:52 |
| Cap | 13 | *16:43 |
| Aqu | 16 | *03:50 |
| Pis | 18 | *11:10 |
| Ari | 20 | *14:21 |
| Tau | 22 | *14:36 |

| 1973 | | |
|---|---|---|
| Vir | 24 | *03:58 |
| Lib | 26 | *08:00 |
| Sco | 28 | *14:18 |
| Sag | 30 | *23:48 |
| Cap | 3 | *12:02 |
| Aqu | 6 | *00:47 |
| Pis | 8 | *11:22 |
| Ari | 10 | *18:28 |
| Tau | 12 | *22:35 |
| Gem | 15 | *01:08 |
| Can | 17 | *03:28 |
| Leo | 19 | *06:24 |
| Vir | 21 | *10:19 |

| 1974 | | |
|---|---|---|
| Cap | 23 | *07:21 |
| Aqu | 25 | *19:38 |
| Pis | 28 | *08:14 |
| Ari | 30 | *19:25 |
| Tau | 3 | *04:38 |
| Gem | 5 | *11:59 |
| Can | 7 | *17:29 |
| Leo | 9 | *21:02 |
| Vir | 11 | *22:55 |
| Lib | 14 | *00:11 |
| Sco | 16 | *02:24 |
| Sag | 18 | *07:14 |
| Cap | 20 | *15:44 |

## ♎ Libra – Finding Your Moon Sign ☽

| 1975 | | | 1976 | | | 1977 | | | 1978 | | | 1979 | | |
|---|---|---|---|---|---|---|---|---|---|---|---|---|---|---|
| Tau | 23 | *06:43 | Lib | 23 | *18:27 | Pis | 24 | *18:29 | Can | 24 | *03:31 | Sco | 24 | *01:53 |
| Gem | 25 | *18:12 | Sco | 25 | *18:33 | Ari | 27 | *00:41 | Leo | 26 | *16:01 | Sag | 26 | *11:34 |
| Can | 28 | *03:05 | Sag | 27 | *19:21 | Tau | 29 | *09:21 | Vir | 29 | *04:10 | Cap | 28 | *18:39 |
| Leo | 30 | *08:19 | Cap | 29 | *22:14 | Gem | 1 | *20:33 | Lib | 1 | *14:15 | Aqu | 30 | *22:47 |
| Vir | 2 | *10:02 | Aqu | 2 | *03:49 | Can | 4 | *09:08 | Sco | 3 | *21:47 | Pis | 3 | *00:22 |
| Lib | 4 | *09:38 | Pis | 4 | *12:10 | Leo | 6 | *20:56 | Sag | 6 | *03:06 | Ari | 5 | *00:28 |
| Sco | 6 | *09:09 | Ari | 6 | *22:50 | Vir | 9 | *05:58 | Cap | 8 | *06:52 | Tau | 7 | *00:45 |
| Sag | 8 | *10:36 | Tau | 9 | *11:11 | Lib | 11 | *11:28 | Aqu | 10 | *09:42 | Gem | 9 | *03:08 |
| Cap | 10 | *15:29 | Gem | 12 | *00:14 | Sco | 13 | *14:10 | Pis | 12 | *12:12 | Can | 11 | *09:10 |
| Aqu | 13 | *00:10 | Can | 14 | *12:22 | Sag | 15 | *15:27 | Ari | 14 | *15:06 | Leo | 13 | *19:11 |
| Pis | 15 | *11:40 | Leo | 16 | *21:48 | Cap | 17 | *16:50 | Tau | 16 | *19:22 | Vir | 16 | *07:51 |
| Ari | 18 | *00:19 | Vir | 19 | *03:23 | Aqu | 19 | *19:36 | Gem | 19 | *02:06 | Lib | 18 | *20:43 |
| Tau | 20 | *12:42 | Lib | 21 | *05:26 | Pis | 22 | *00:27 | Can | 21 | *11:53 | Sco | 21 | *08:01 |
| Gem | 22 | *23:50 | | | | | | | | | | | | |

♎ Libra – Finding Your Moon Sign ☽

| 1980 | | |
|---|---|---|
| Ari | 24 | *09:36 |
| Tau | 26 | *08:53 |
| Gem | 28 | *09:21 |
| Can | 30 | *12:47 |
| Leo | 2 | *19:57 |
| Vir | 5 | *06:18 |
| Lib | 7 | *18:30 |
| Sco | 10 | *07:14 |
| Sag | 12 | *19:37 |
| Cap | 15 | *06:36 |
| Aqu | 17 | *14:52 |
| Pis | 19 | *19:30 |
| Ari | 21 | *20:42 |

| 1981 | | |
|---|---|---|
| Leo | 23 | *04:08 |
| Vir | 25 | *10:29 |
| Lib | 27 | *18:40 |
| Sco | 30 | *04:52 |
| Sag | 2 | *16:59 |
| Cap | 5 | *05:48 |
| Aqu | 7 | *17:00 |
| Pis | 10 | *00:30 |
| Ari | 12 | *04:00 |
| Tau | 14 | *04:42 |
| Gem | 16 | *04:41 |
| Can | 18 | *05:52 |
| Leo | 20 | *09:35 |
| Vir | 22 | *16:05 |

| 1982 | | |
|---|---|---|
| Cap | 25 | *00:31 |
| Aqu | 27 | *13:20 |
| Pis | 30 | *00:17 |
| Ari | 2 | *08:05 |
| Tau | 4 | *13:08 |
| Gem | 6 | *16:38 |
| Can | 8 | *19:39 |
| Leo | 10 | *22:44 |
| Vir | 13 | *02:09 |
| Lib | 15 | *06:22 |
| Sco | 17 | *12:21 |
| Sag | 19 | *21:03 |
| Cap | 22 | *08:38 |

| 1983 | | |
|---|---|---|
| Tau | 24 | *19:12 |
| Gem | 27 | *03:23 |
| Can | 29 | *09:23 |
| Leo | 1 | *12:53 |
| Vir | 3 | *14:14 |
| Lib | 5 | *14:41 |
| Sco | 7 | *16:06 |
| Sag | 9 | *20:21 |
| Cap | 12 | *04:30 |
| Aqu | 14 | *16:00 |
| Pis | 17 | *04:41 |
| Ari | 19 | *16:18 |
| Tau | 22 | *01:46 |

| 1984 | | |
|---|---|---|
| Vir | 23 | *00:17 |
| Lib | 24 | *23:40 |
| Sco | 26 | *23:04 |
| Sag | 29 | *00:33 |
| Cap | 1 | *05:27 |
| Aqu | 3 | *14:03 |
| Pis | 6 | *01:19 |
| Ari | 8 | *13:50 |
| Tau | 11 | *02:27 |
| Gem | 13 | *14:13 |
| Can | 15 | *23:58 |
| Leo | 18 | *06:40 |
| Vir | 20 | *09:54 |
| Lib | 22 | *10:31 |

♎ Libra – Finding Your Moon Sign ☽

| 1985 | | |
|---|---|---|
| Aqu | 23 | *19:11 |
| Pis | 26 | *02:50 |
| Ari | 28 | *12:43 |
| Tau | 1 | *00:35 |
| Gem | 3 | *13:36 |
| Can | 6 | *01:58 |
| Leo | 8 | *11:32 |
| Vir | 10 | *17:09 |
| Lib | 12 | *19:11 |
| Sco | 14 | *19:12 |
| Sag | 16 | *19:05 |
| Cap | 18 | *20:35 |
| Aqu | 21 | *00:55 |

| 1986 | | |
|---|---|---|
| Gem | 23 | *09:13 |
| Can | 25 | *21:44 |
| Leo | 28 | *09:38 |
| Vir | 30 | *18:57 |
| Lib | 3 | *01:01 |
| Sco | 5 | *04:34 |
| Sag | 7 | *06:47 |
| Cap | 9 | *08:52 |
| Aqu | 11 | *11:45 |
| Pis | 13 | *16:03 |
| Ari | 15 | *22:13 |
| Tau | 18 | *06:35 |
| Gem | 20 | *17:15 |

| 1987 | | |
|---|---|---|
| Lib | 23 | *03:57 |
| Sco | 25 | *12:29 |
| Sag | 27 | *18:48 |
| Cap | 29 | *23:07 |
| Aqu | 2 | *01:50 |
| Pis | 4 | *03:39 |
| Ari | 6 | *05:34 |
| Tau | 8 | *08:58 |
| Gem | 10 | *15:04 |
| Can | 13 | *00:31 |
| Leo | 15 | *12:34 |
| Vir | 18 | *01:05 |
| Lib | 20 | *11:48 |
| Sco | 22 | *19:41 |

| 1988 | | |
|---|---|---|
| Pis | 23 | *14:50 |
| Ari | 25 | *14:29 |
| Tau | 27 | *14:29 |
| Gem | 29 | *16:43 |
| Can | 1 | *22:39 |
| Leo | 4 | *08:31 |
| Vir | 6 | *21:01 |
| Lib | 9 | *10:03 |
| Sco | 11 | *21:57 |
| Sag | 14 | *07:57 |
| Cap | 16 | *15:43 |
| Aqu | 18 | *21:04 |
| Pis | 20 | *23:57 |

| 1989 | | |
|---|---|---|
| Leo | 24 | *10:45 |
| Vir | 26 | *20:32 |
| Lib | 29 | *08:14 |
| Sco | 1 | *20:52 |
| Sag | 4 | *09:28 |
| Cap | 6 | *20:44 |
| Aqu | 9 | *05:06 |
| Pis | 11 | *09:36 |
| Ari | 13 | *10:40 |
| Tau | 15 | *09:52 |
| Gem | 17 | *09:19 |
| Can | 19 | *11:10 |
| Leo | 21 | *16:47 |

## ♎ Libra – Finding Your Moon Sign ☽

| 1990 | | |
|---|---|---|
| Sag | 24 | *05:52 |
| Cap | 26 | *18:36 |
| Aqu | 29 | *05:53 |
| Pis | 1 | *13:40 |
| Ari | 3 | *17:41 |
| Tau | 5 | *19:05 |
| Gem | 7 | *19:47 |
| Can | 9 | *21:30 |
| Leo | 12 | *01:17 |
| Vir | 14 | *07:20 |
| Lib | 16 | *15:26 |
| Sco | 19 | *01:24 |
| Sag | 21 | *13:09 |

| 1991 | | |
|---|---|---|
| Ari | 23 | *21:54 |
| Tau | 26 | *03:58 |
| Gem | 28 | *08:25 |
| Can | 30 | *11:57 |
| Leo | 2 | *14:58 |
| Vir | 4 | *17:44 |
| Lib | 6 | *21:00 |
| Sco | 9 | *02:00 |
| Sag | 11 | *09:58 |
| Cap | 13 | *21:10 |
| Aqu | 16 | *10:04 |
| Pis | 18 | *21:51 |
| Ari | 21 | *06:32 |

| 1992 | | |
|---|---|---|
| Vir | 24 | *05:07 |
| Lib | 26 | *04:55 |
| Sco | 28 | *05:44 |
| Sag | 30 | *09:34 |
| Cap | 2 | *17:29 |
| Aqu | 5 | *04:52 |
| Pis | 7 | *17:37 |
| Ari | 10 | *05:35 |
| Tau | 12 | *15:47 |
| Gem | 15 | *00:07 |
| Can | 17 | *06:35 |
| Leo | 19 | *11:00 |
| Vir | 21 | *13:26 |

| 1993 | | |
|---|---|---|
| Aqu | 25 | *04:19 |
| Pis | 27 | *15:13 |
| Ari | 30 | *03:28 |
| Tau | 2 | *16:13 |
| Gem | 5 | *04:26 |
| Can | 7 | *14:41 |
| Leo | 9 | *21:32 |
| Vir | 12 | *00:34 |
| Lib | 14 | *00:46 |
| Sco | 16 | *00:01 |
| Sag | 18 | *00:24 |
| Cap | 20 | *03:42 |
| Aqu | 22 | *10:50 |

| 1994 | | |
|---|---|---|
| Gem | 25 | *02:41 |
| Can | 27 | *15:11 |
| Leo | 30 | *00:53 |
| Vir | 2 | *06:39 |
| Lib | 4 | *08:55 |
| Sco | 6 | *09:21 |
| Sag | 8 | *09:47 |
| Cap | 10 | *11:44 |
| Aqu | 12 | *16:09 |
| Pis | 14 | *23:18 |
| Ari | 17 | *08:56 |
| Tau | 19 | *20:34 |
| Gem | 22 | *09:27 |

## ♎ Libra – Finding Your Moon Sign ☽

| 1995 | | |
|---|---|---|
| Lib | 24 | *14:48 |
| Sco | 26 | *19:19 |
| Sag | 28 | *22:30 |
| Cap | 1 | *01:10 |
| Aqu | 3 | *03:59 |
| Pis | 5 | *07:35 |
| Ari | 7 | *12:42 |
| Tau | 9 | *20:05 |
| Gem | 12 | *06:09 |
| Can | 14 | *18:19 |
| Leo | 17 | *06:46 |
| Vir | 19 | *17:11 |
| Lib | 22 | *00:13 |

| 1996 | | |
|---|---|---|
| Pis | 24 | *18:42 |
| Ari | 26 | *19:45 |
| Tau | 28 | *22:24 |
| Gem | 1 | *04:02 |
| Can | 3 | *13:15 |
| Leo | 6 | *01:11 |
| Vir | 8 | *13:48 |
| Lib | 11 | *00:59 |
| Sco | 13 | *09:44 |
| Sag | 15 | *16:06 |
| Cap | 17 | *20:36 |
| Aqu | 19 | *23:50 |
| Pis | 22 | *02:21 |

| 1997 | | |
|---|---|---|
| Can | 23 | *12:34 |
| Leo | 25 | *22:13 |
| Vir | 28 | *10:27 |
| Lib | 30 | *23:31 |
| Sco | 3 | *11:56 |
| Sag | 5 | *22:41 |
| Cap | 8 | *07:03 |
| Aqu | 10 | *12:27 |
| Pis | 12 | *14:58 |
| Ari | 14 | *15:24 |
| Tau | 16 | *15:16 |
| Gem | 18 | *16:26 |
| Can | 20 | *20:46 |

| 1998 | | |
|---|---|---|
| Sco | 23 | *10:21 |
| Sag | 25 | *23:04 |
| Cap | 28 | *10:29 |
| Aqu | 30 | *18:52 |
| Pis | 2 | *23:21 |
| Ari | 5 | *00:31 |
| Tau | 6 | *23:57 |
| Gem | 8 | *23:44 |
| Can | 11 | *01:49 |
| Leo | 13 | *07:25 |
| Vir | 15 | *16:32 |
| Lib | 18 | *04:02 |
| Sco | 20 | *16:36 |

| 1999 | | |
|---|---|---|
| Pis | 23 | *02:50 |
| Ari | 25 | *07:33 |
| Tau | 27 | *09:50 |
| Gem | 29 | *11:21 |
| Can | 1 | *13:31 |
| Leo | 3 | *17:13 |
| Vir | 5 | *22:40 |
| Lib | 8 | *05:51 |
| Sco | 10 | *15:01 |
| Sag | 13 | *02:18 |
| Cap | 15 | *15:03 |
| Aqu | 18 | *03:16 |
| Pis | 20 | *12:31 |
| Ari | 22 | *17:41 |

| 2000 | | |
|---|---|---|
| Leo | 23 | *06:59 |
| Vir | 25 | *09:01 |
| Lib | 27 | *11:22 |
| Sco | 29 | *15:30 |
| Sag | 1 | *22:50 |
| Cap | 4 | *09:42 |
| Aqu | 6 | *22:32 |
| Pis | 9 | *10:35 |
| Ari | 11 | *19:50 |
| Tau | 14 | *02:05 |
| Gem | 16 | *06:18 |
| Can | 18 | *09:36 |
| Leo | 20 | *12:42 |
| Vir | 22 | *15:52 |

## ♎ Libra Mercury Signs ☿

| YEAR | VIRGO | LIBRA | SCORPIO |
|------|-------|-------|---------|
| 1930 | 22 Sep–11 Oct | 11 Oct–23 Oct | |
| 1931 | 22 Sep–4 Oct | 4 Oct–23 Oct | 23 Oct |
| 1932 | 22 Sep–26 Sep | 26 Sep–13 Oct | 13 Oct–23 Oct |
| 1933 | | 22 Sep–6 Oct | 6 Oct–23 Oct |
| 1934 | | 22 Sep–30 Sep | 30 Sep–23 Oct |
| 1935 | | 22 Sep–28 Sep | 28 Sep–12 Oct |
| | | 12 Oct–23 Oct | |
| 1936 | | 22 Sep–23 Oct | |
| 1937 | 22 Sep–8 Oct | 8 Oct–23 Oct | |
| 1938 | 23 Sep–1 Oct | 1 Oct–18 Oct | 18 Oct–24 Oct |
| 1939 | | 23 Sep–11 Oct | 11 Oct–23 Oct |
| 1940 | | 22 Sep–3 Oct | 3 Oct–23 Oct |
| 1941 | | 22 Sep–28 Sep | 28 Sep–23 Oct |
| 1942 | | 22 Sep–23 Oct | |
| 1943 | | 22 Sep–25 Sep | 25 Sep–11 Oct |
| | | 11 Oct–23 Oct | |
| 1944 | 22 Sep–5 Oct | 5 Oct–23 Oct | 23 Oct |
| 1945 | 23 Sep–27 Sep | 27 Sep–15 Oct | 15 Oct–23 Oct |
| 1946 | | 22 Sep–1 Oct | 1 Oct–23 Oct |
| 1947 | | 22 Sep–1 Oct | 1 Oct–23 Oct |
| 1948 | | 22 Sep–27 Sep | 27 Sep–17 Oct |
| 1949 | | 17 Oct–23 Oct | |
| 1950 | 22 Sep–9 Oct | 9 Oct–23 Oct | |
| 1951 | 22 Sep–2 Oct | 2 Oct–19 Oct | 19 Oct–23 Oct |
| 1952 | 22 Sep–11 Oct | 11 Oct–23 Oct | |
| 1953 | | 22 Sep–4 Oct | 4 Oct–23 Oct |
| 1954 | | 22 Sep–29 Sep | 29 Sep–23 Oct |
| 1955 | | 22 Sep–23 Oct | |

| YEAR | VIRGO | LIBRA | SCORPIO |
|---|---|---|---|
| 1956 | 22 Sep–29 Sep | 29 Sep–11 Oct | |
| | | 11 Oct–23 Oct | |
| 1957 | 22 Sep–6 Oct | 6 Oct–23 Oct | |
| 1958 | 22 Sep–28 Sep | 28 Sep–16 Oct | 16 Oct–23 Oct |
| 1959 | | 22 Sep–9 Oct | 9 Oct–23 Oct |
| 1960 | | 22 Sep–1 Oct | 1 Oct–23 Oct |
| 1961 | | 22 Sep–27 Sep | 27 Sep–22 Oct |
| | | 22 Oct– 23 Oct | |
| 1962 | | 22 Sep–23 Oct | |
| 1963 | 22 Sep–10 Oct | 10 Oct–23 Oct | |
| 1964 | 22 Sep–3 Oct | 3 Oct–20 Oct | 20 Oct- 23 Oct |
| 1965 | 22 Sep–25 Sep | 25 Sep–12 Oct | 12 Oct–23 Oct |
| 1966 | | 22 Sep–5 Oct | 5 Oct–23 Oct |
| 1967 | | 22 Sep–30 Sep | 30 Sep–23 Oct |
| 1968 | | 22 Sep–28 Sep | 28 Sep–7 Oct |
| | | 7 Oct–23 Oct | |
| 1969 | 7 Oct–9 Oct | 23 Sep–7 Oct | |
| | | 9 Oct–23 Oct | |
| 1970 | 22 Sep–7 Oct | 7 Oct–23 Oct | |
| 1971 | 22 Sep–30 Sep | 30 Sep–17 Oct | 17 Oct–23 Oct |
| 1972 | | 22 Sep–9 Oct | 9 Oct–23 Oct |
| 1973 | | 22 Sep–2 Oct | 2 Oct–23 Oct |
| 1974 | | 22 Sep–28 Sep | 28 Sep–23 Oct |
| 1975 | | 22 Sep–23 Oct | |
| 1976 | 22 Sep–10 Oct | 10 Oct–23 Oct | |
| 1977 | 22 Sep–4 Oct | 4 Oct–21 Oct | 21 Oct–23 Oct |
| 1978 | 22 Sep–26 Sep | 26 Sep–14 Oct | 14 Oct–23 Oct |
| 1979 | | 22 Sep–7 Oct | 7 Oct–23 Oct |
| 1980 | | 22 Sep–30 Sep | 30 Sep–23 Oct |
| 1981 | | 22 Sep–27 Sep | 27 Sep–14 Oct |
| | | 14 Oct–23 Oct | |
| 1982 | | 22 Sep–23 Oct | |

| YEAR | VIRGO | LIBRA | SCORPIO |
|------|-------|-------|---------|
| 1983 | 22 Sep–8 Oct | 8 Oct–23 Oct | |
| 1984 | 22 Sep–30 Sep | 30 Sep–18 Oct | 18 Oct–23 Oct |
| 1985 | | 22 Sep–10 Oct | 10 Oct–23 Oct |
| 1986 | | 22 Sep–4 Oct | 4 Oct–23 Oct |
| 1987 | | 22 Sep–28 Sep | 28 Sep–23 Oct |
| 1988 | | 22 Sep–23 Oct | |
| 1989 | | 26 Sep–11 Oct | 22 Sep–26 Sep |
| | | 11 Oct–23 Oct | |
| 1990 | 22 Sep–5 Oct | 5 Oct–23 Oct | |
| 1991 | 22 Sep–28 Sep | 28 Sep–15 Oct | 15 Oct–23 Oct |
| 1992 | | 22 Sep–7 Oct | 7 Oct–23 Oct |
| 1993 | | 22 Sep–1 Oct | 1 Oct–23 Oct |
| 1994 | | 22 Sep–27 Sep | 27 Sep–19 Oct |
| | | 19 Oct–23 Oct | |
| 1995 | | 22 Sep–23 Oct | |
| 1996 | 22 Sep–9 Oct | 9 Oct–23 Oct | |
| 1997 | 22 Sep–2 Oct | 2 Oct–19 Oct | 19 Oct–23 Oct |
| 1998 | 22 Sep–2 Oct | 2 Oct–19 Oct | 19 Oct–23 Oct |
| 1999 | | 22 Sep–5 Oct | 5 Oct–23 Oct |
| 2000 | | 22 Sep–28 Sep | 28 Sep–23 Oct |

## ♎ Libra Venus Signs ♀

| YEAR | LEO | VIRGO | LIBRA | SCORPIO | SAGITTARIUS |
|------|-----|-------|-------|---------|-------------|
| 1930 | | | | 23 Sep–12 Oct | 12 Oct–24 Oct |
| 1931 | | | 23 Sep–14 Oct | 14 Oct–24 Oct | |
| 1932 | 23 Sep–7 Oct | 7 Oct–24 Oct | | | |
| 1933 | | 23 Sep–5 Oct | 5 Oct–24 Oct | | |
| 1934 | | 23 Sep–24 Oct | | | |
| 1935 | | | | 23 Sep–11 Oct | 11 Oct–24 Oct |
| 1936 | | | 23 Sep–28 Sep | 28 Sep–23 Oct | 23 Oct–24 Oct |
| 1937 | 23 Sep–25 Sep | 25 Sep–19 Oct | 19 Oct–24 Oct | | |
| 1938 | | | | 23 Sep–13 Oct | 13 Oct–24 Oct |
| 1939 | | | 23 Sep–14 Oct | 14 Oct–24 Oct | |
| 1940 | 23 Sep–6 Oct | 6 Oct–24 Oct | | | |
| 1941 | | 23 Sep–4 Oct | 4 Oct–24 Oct | | |
| 1942 | | 23 Sep–24 Oct | | | |
| 1943 | | | | 23 Sep–10 Oct | 10 Oct–24 Oct |
| 1944 | | | 23 Sep–28 Sep | 28 Sep–22 Oct | 22 Oct–24 Oct |
| 1945 | 23 Sep–24 Sep | 24 Sep–19 Oct | 19 Oct–24 Oct | | |
| 1946 | | | | 23 Sep–16 Oct | 16 Oct–24 Oct |
| 1947 | | | 23 Sep–13 Oct | 13 Oct–24 Oct | |
| 1948 | 23 Sep–6 Oct | 6 Oct–24 Oct | | | |
| 1949 | | 23 Sep–4 Oct | 4 Oct–24 Oct | | |
| 1950 | | 23 Sep–24 Oct | | | |
| 1951 | | | | 23 Sep–10 Oct | 10 Oct–24 Oct |

| YEAR | LEO | VIRGO | LIBRA | SCORPIO | SAGITTARIUS |
|------|-----|-------|-------|---------|-------------|
| 1952 | | | 23 Sep–27 Sep | 27 Sep–22 Oct | 22 Oct–24 Oct |
| 1953 | 23 Sep–24 Sep | 24 Sep–18 Oct | 18 Oct–24 Oct | | |
| 1954 | | | | 23 Sep–24 Oct | |
| 1955 | | | 23 Sep–13 Oct | 13 Oct–24 Oct | |
| 1956 | 23 Sep–6 Oct | 6 Oct–24 Oct | | | |
| 1957 | | 23 Sep–3 Oct | 3 Oct–24 Oct | | |
| 1958 | | | | 23 Sep–10 Oct | 10 Oct–24 Oct |
| 1959 | 23 Sep–25 Sep | 25 Sep–24 Oct | | | |
| 1960 | | | 23 Sep–27 Sep | 27 Sep–21 Oct | 21 Oct–24 Oct |
| 1961 | 23 Sep | 23 Sep–18 Oct | 18 Oct–24 Oct | | |
| 1962 | | | | 23 Sep–24 Oct | |
| 1963 | 23 Sep–5 Oct | 5 Oct–24 Oct | | | |
| 1964 | | | 23 Sep–12 Oct | 12 Oct–24 Oct | |
| 1965 | | 23 Sep–3 Oct | 3 Oct–24 Oct | | |
| 1966 | | | | 23 Sep–9 Oct | 9 Oct–24 Oct |
| 1967 | 23 Sep–1 Oct | 1 Oct–24 Oct | | | |
| 1968 | | | 22 Sep–26 Sep | 26 Sep–21 Oct | 21 Oct–24 Oct |
| 1969 | 23 Sep | 23 Sep–17 Oct | 17 Oct–24 Oct | | |
| 1970 | | | | 23 Sep–24 Oct | |
| 1971 | 22 Sep–5 Oct | 5 Oct–24 Oct | | | |
| 1972 | | | 23 Sep–11 Oct | 11 Oct–24 Oct | |
| 1973 | | 23 Sep–2 Oct | 2 Oct–24 Oct | | |
| 1974 | | | | 23 Sep–9 Oct | 9 Oct–24 Oct |
| 1975 | 23 Sep–4 Oct | 4 Oct–24 Oct | | | |
| 1976 | | | 22 Sep–26 Sep | 26 Sep–20 Oct | 20 Oct–24 Oct |

| YEAR | LEO | VIRGO | LIBRA | SCORPIO | SAGITTARIUS |
|---|---|---|---|---|---|
| 1977 | | 23 Sep–17 Oct | 17 Oct–24 Oct | 23 Sep–24 Oct | |
| 1978 | | | | 11 Oct–24 Oct | |
| 1979 | | | 23 Sep–11 Oct | | |
| 1980 | 22 Sep–4 Oct | 4 Oct–24 Oct | | 23 Sep–9 Oct | 9 Oct–24 Oct |
| 1981 | | | 2 Oct–24 Oct | | |
| 1982 | | 23 Sep–2 Oct | | | |
| 1983 | 23 Sep–5 Oct | 5 Oct–24 Oct | | | |
| 1984 | | | 22 Sep–25 Sep | 25 Sep–20 Oct | 20 Oct–24 Oct |
| 1985 | | | 16 Oct–24 Oct | | |
| 1986 | | 23 Sep–16 Oct | | 23 Sep–24 Oct | |
| 1987 | | | 23 Sep–10 Oct | 10 Oct–24 Oct | |
| 1988 | 22 Sep–4 Oct | 4 Oct–24 Oct | | | |
| 1989 | | | | 23 Sep–8 Oct | 8 Oct–24 Oct |
| 1990 | | 23 Sep–1 Oct | 1 Oct–24 Oct | | |
| 1991 | 23 Sep–6 Oct | 6 Oct–24 Oct | | | |
| 1992 | | | 22 Sep–25 Sep | 25 Sep–19 Oct | 19 Oct–24 Oct |
| 1993 | | 23 Sep–16 Oct | 16 Oct–24 Oct | | |
| 1994 | | | | 23 Sep–24 Oct | |
| 1995 | | | 23 Sep–10 Oct | 10 Oct–24 Oct | |
| 1996 | 23 Sep–4 Oct | 4 Oct–24 Oct | | | |
| 1997 | | | | 22 Sep–8 Oct | 8 Oct–24 Oct |
| 1998 | | 23 Sep–30 Sep | 30 Sep–24 Oct | | |
| 1999 | 23 Sep–7 Oct | 7 Oct–24 Oct | | | |
| 2000 | | | 22 Sep–24 Sep | 24 Sep–19 Oct | 19 Oct–24 Oct |

# The Libra Workbook

There are no right or wrong answers in this chapter. Its aim is to help you assess how you are doing with your life – in YOUR estimation – and to make the material of this book more personal and, I hope, more helpful for you.

### 1. The Libra in You
Which of the following Libran characteristics do you recognise in yourself?

| | | |
|---|---|---|
| charming | cooperative | courteous |
| diplomatic | elegant | fair |
| gracious | harmonious | peacemaking |
| strategic | principled | romantic |

### 2. In which situations do you find yourself acting like this?
_____

_____

### 3. When you are feeling vulnerable, you may show some of the less constructive Libran traits. Do you recognise yourself in any of the following?

| | | |
|---|---|---|
| naive | vain | over-idealistic |
| scheming | placating | lazy |
| indecisive | weak-willed | frivolous |

What kind of situations trigger off this behaviour and what do you think might help you, in these situations, to respond more positively?

_____

_____


## 4. You and Your Roles
a) Where, if anywhere, in your life do you play the role of Architect?

_____

_____

b) What do you plan to achieve?

_____

_____

5. Do you play any of the following roles – in the literal or broad sense – in any part of your life? If not, would you like to? What might be your first step towards doing so?

Designer        Partner        Political activist
Advocate        Diplomat       Judge

_____

_____


## 6. Sun Aspects
If any of the following planets aspects your Sun, add each of the keywords for that planet to complete the following sentences. Which phrases ring true for you?

I am _____
My father is_____
My job requires that I am_____

## Saturn Words (Use only if your Sun is aspected by Saturn)

| | | | |
|---|---|---|---|
| ambitious | controlling | judgmental | mature |
| serious | strict | traditional | bureaucratic |
| cautious | committed | hard-working | disciplined |
| depressive | responsible | status-seeking | limiting |

## Uranus Words (Use only if your Sun is aspected by Uranus)

| | | | |
|---|---|---|---|
| freedom-loving | progressive | rebellious | shocking |
| scientific | cutting-edge | detached | contrary |
| friendly | disruptive | eccentric | humanitarian |
| innovative | nonconformist | unconventional | exciting |

## Neptune Words (Use only if your Sun is aspected by Neptune)

| | | | |
|---|---|---|---|
| sensitive | idealistic | artistic | impressionable |
| disappointing | impractical | escapist | self-sacrificing |
| spiritual | unrealistic | dreamy | glamorous |
| dependent | deceptive | rescuing | blissful |

## Pluto Words (Use only if your Sun is aspected by Pluto)

| | | | |
|---|---|---|---|
| powerful | single-minded | intense | extreme |
| secretive | rotten | passionate | mysterious |
| investigative | uncompromising | ruthless | wealthy |
| abusive | regenerative | associated with sex, birth or death | |

a) If one or more negative words describe you or your job, how might you turn that quality into something more positive or satisfying?

_____

_____

## 7. The Moon and You

Below are brief lists of what the Moon needs, in the various elements, to feel secure and satisfied. First find your Moon element, then estimate how much of each of the following you are expressing and receiving in your life, especially at home and in your relationships, on a scale of 0 to 5 where 0 = none and 5 = plenty.

### FIRE MOONS – Aries, Leo, Sagittarius

| | | |
|---|---|---|
| attention | action | drama |
| recognition | self-expression | spontaneity |
| enthusiasm | adventure | leadership |

### EARTH MOONS – Taurus, Virgo, Capricorn

| | | |
|---|---|---|
| stability | orderly routine | sensual pleasures |
| material security | a sense of rootedness | control over your home life |
| regular body care | practical achievements | pleasurable practical tasks |

### AIR MOONS – Gemini, Libra, Aquarius

| | | |
|---|---|---|
| mental rapport | stimulating ideas | emotional space |
| friendship | social justice | interesting conversations |
| fairness | socialising | freedom to circulate |

### WATER MOONS – Cancer, Scorpio, Pisces

| | | |
|---|---|---|
| intimacy | a sense of belonging | emotional rapport |
| emotional safety | respect for your feelings | time and space to retreat |
| acceptance | cherishing and being cherished | warmth and comfort |

a) Do you feel your Moon is being 'fed' enough?

yes_____     no_____

b) How might you satisfy your Moon needs even better?

_____

_____


## 8. You and Your Mercury

As a Libran, your Mercury can only be in Virgo, Libra or Scorpio. Below are some of the ways and situations in which Mercury in each of the elements might learn and communicate effectively. First find your Mercury sign, then circle the words you think apply to you.

**Mercury in Fire** (As a Libran, you can never have Mercury in a fire sign; the words are included here for completeness)

| | | |
|---|---|---|
| action | imagination | identifying with the subject matter |
| excitement | drama | playing with possibilities |

### Mercury in Earth (Virgo)

| | | |
|---|---|---|
| time-tested methods | useful facts | well-structured information |
| 'how to' instructions | demonstrations | hands-on experience |

### Mercury in Air (Libra)

| | | |
|---|---|---|
| facts arranged in categories | logic | demonstrable connections |
| rational arguments | theories | debate and sharing of ideas |

### Mercury in Water (Scorpio)

| | | |
|---|---|---|
| pictures and images | charged atmospheres | feeling-linked information |
| intuitive understanding | emotional rapport | being shown personally |

a) This game with Mercury can be done with a friend or on

your own. Skim through a magazine until you find a picture that interests you. Then describe the picture – to your friend, or in writing or on tape. Notice what you emphasise and the kind of words you use. Now try to describe it using the language and emphasis of each of the other Mercury modes. How easy did you find that? Identifying the preferred Mercury style of others and using that style yourself can lead to improved communication all round.

## 9. Your Venus Values

Below are lists of qualities and situations that your Venus sign might enjoy. Assess on a scale of 0 to 5 how much your Venus desires and pleasures are met and expressed in your life. 0 = not at all, 5 = fully.

### Venus in Leo

You will activate your Venus through anything that makes you feel special, unique, radiant and generous, for example:

extravagant gestures      luxury goods      prestigious activities
being central in a drama   acting nobly      being in love

### Venus in Virgo

You will activate your Venus through anything that engages your powers of discrimination, for example:

restoring order           improving efficiency   using your skills
purifying your mind,       being of service       quality work
body or environment

## Venus in Libra
You will activate your Venus through anything cultured, balanced and fair, for example:

| | | |
|---|---|---|
| harmonious relationships | elegant surroundings | dressing well |
| courteous manners | artistic pursuits | political justice |

## Venus in Scorpio
You will activate your Venus through anything that allows you to penetrate to the heart of life's mysteries, for example:

| | | |
|---|---|---|
| survival situations | money, power and sex | investigating secrets |
| transformative experiences | recycling | intense relationships |

## Venus in Sagittarius
You will activate your Venus through following your adventurous spirit, opening up new frontiers and sharing your enthusiasm with others, for example:

| | | |
|---|---|---|
| travelling | sport | searching for the meaning of life |
| teaching or preaching | inspiring others | publishing or broadcasting |

a) How, and where, might you have more fun and pleasure by bringing more of what your Venus sign loves into your life?

_____

_____

b) Make a note here of the kind of gifts your Venus sign would love to receive. Then go on and spoil yourself . . .

_____

_____

# Resources

### Finding an Astrologer

I'm often asked what is the best way to find a reputable astrologer. Personal recommendation by someone whose judgement you trust is by far the best way. Ideally, the astrologer should also be endorsed by a reputable organisation whose members adhere to a strict code of ethics, which guarantees confidentiality and professional conduct.

### Contact Addresses

Association of Professional Astrologers International
www.professionalastrologers.org
   APAI members adhere to a strict code of professional ethics.

Astrological Association of Great Britain
www.astrologicalassociation.co.uk
   The main body for astrology in the UK, with links to similar organisations throughout the world.

Faculty of Astrological Studies
www.astrology.org.uk
   The teaching body internationally recognised for excellence in astrological education at all levels.

Jane Ridder-Patrick
*www.janeridderpatrick.com*

# Your Libran Friends

You can keep a record of Librans you know here, with the page numbers of where to find their descriptions handy for future reference.

Name _____  Date of Birth _____

| Aspects* | None | Saturn | Uranus | Neptune | Pluto |
|----------|------|--------|--------|---------|-------|
| Moon Sign _____ | | | | p _____ | |
| Mercury Sign _____ | | | | p _____ | |
| Venus Sign _____ | | | | p _____ | |

Name _____  Date of Birth _____

| Aspects* | None | Saturn | Uranus | Neptune | Pluto |
|----------|------|--------|--------|---------|-------|
| Moon Sign _____ | | | | p _____ | |
| Mercury Sign _____ | | | | p _____ | |
| Venus Sign _____ | | | | p _____ | |

Name _____  Date of Birth _____

| Aspects* | None | Saturn | Uranus | Neptune | Pluto |
|----------|------|--------|--------|---------|-------|
| Moon Sign _____ | | | | p _____ | |
| Mercury Sign _____ | | | | p _____ | |
| Venus Sign _____ | | | | p _____ | |

Name _____  Date of Birth _____

| Aspects* | None | Saturn | Uranus | Neptune | Pluto |
|----------|------|--------|--------|---------|-------|
| Moon Sign _____ | | | | p _____ | |
| Mercury Sign _____ | | | | p _____ | |
| Venus Sign _____ | | | | p _____ | |

* Circle where applicable

## Sign Summaries

| SIGN | GLYPH | APPROX DATES | SYMBOL | ROLE | ELEMENT | QUALITY | PLANET | GLYPH | KEYWORD |
|------|-------|--------------|--------|------|---------|---------|--------|-------|---------|
| 1. Aries | ♈ | 21/3 – 19/4 | Ram | Hero | Fire | Cardinal | Mars | ♂ | Assertiveness |
| 2. Taurus | ♉ | 20/4 – 20/5 | Bull | Steward | Earth | Fixed | Venus | ♀ | Stability |
| 3. Gemini | ♊ | 21/5 – 21/6 | Twins | Go-Between | Air | Mutable | Mercury | ☿ | Communication |
| 4. Cancer | ♋ | 22/6 – 22/7 | Crab | Caretaker | Water | Cardinal | Moon | ☽ | Nurture |
| 5. Leo | ♌ | 23/7 – 22/8 | Lion | Performer | Fire | Fixed | Sun | ☉ | Glory |
| 6. Virgo | ♍ | 23/8 – 22/9 | Maiden | Craftworker | Earth | Mutable | Mercury | ☿ | Skill |
| 7. Libra | ♎ | 23/9 – 22/10 | Scales | Architect | Air | Cardinal | Venus | ♀ | Balance |
| 8. Scorpio | ♏ | 23/10 – 23/11 | Scorpion | Survivor | Water | Fixed | Pluto | ♇ | Transformation |
| 9. Sagittarius | ♐ | 22/11 – 21/12 | Archer | Adventurer | Fire | Mutable | Jupiter | ♃ | Wisdom |
| 10. Capricorn | ♑ | 22/12 – 19/1 | Goat | Manager | Earth | Cardinal | Saturn | ♄ | Responsibility |
| 11. Aquarius | ♒ | 20/1 – 19/2 | Waterbearer | Scientist | Air | Fixed | Uranus | ♅ | Progress |
| 12. Pisces | ♓ | 20/2 – 20/3 | Fishes | Dreamer | Water | Mutable | Neptune | ♆ | Universality |